BICYCLES
IN WAR

Military Histories and Studies
by MARTIN CAIDIN

The Tigers Are Burning
The Fork-Tailed Devil
Zero!
Samurai!
The Ragged, Rugged Warriors
Black Thursday
The Long Arm of America
Air Force
Thunderbolt!
Golden Wings
The Zero Fighter
A Torch to the Enemy
The Night Hamburg Died
Flying Forts
Messerschmitt ME-109
The Mission
The Long Night
When War Comes

BICYCLES IN WAR

Martin Caidin

and

Jay Barbree

HAWTHORN BOOKS, INC.
PUBLISHERS/NEW YORK

for
our friend
GEORGE WILSON

629.227
C

Contents

Acknowledgments

Researching this book and its illustrations presented the unusual problem of disturbing dust that hadn't been moved for a long time. The project of digging out the details of the use of bicycles in war invariably provoked glassy-eyed stares of disbelief. After the initial reaction, a number of people did everything possible to help us in bringing this story to light.

We wish especially to thank John J. Slonaker, research historian of the Department of the Army, Military History Research Collection at Carlisle Barracks, Pennsylvania, for many hours spent in researching historical material and photographs.

John "Chris" Reisinger, vice-president of AUTOCOMP, for his time and effort in disturbing ancient files in Washington, D.C., to unearth photographs.

Miss Denise Myhill for spending much time and effort in London, England, especially in the Imperial War Museum, and for her invaluable information and illustrations.

Mr. Robert S. Kohn of the Battelle Memorial Institute, Columbus, Ohio, who was most helpful with his steady supply of historical facts on the military bicycle.

And a kind word to Dame Sybil Leek, Dr. William E. Bagwell, and Edward Hymoff for their assistance.

BICYCLES
IN WAR

1

Death Ride

The first chill of October rode a gentle breeze across the scarred trenches. The wind carried to Pvt. Henri Roget with its stink of burnt powder. The French soldier sniffed and wrinkled his nose with distaste, for the wind also bore the smell of death.

Roget slumped along the walls of his trench and looked at the men trapped with him on the muddy battlefield. The soldiers in the 5th Infantry of the French Army had huddled low in their trenches since first light, pinned to sticky mud by an unending rain of German artillery and mortar shells. They were in a race for time. A reinforcement column of two thousand men was on its way. Would it reach them before the Germans opened the final assault on the trenches?

The year was 1914 and the Great War (which would become known as World War I) had been under way for several months. But terrible battles were already decimating the armies of both sides. On the northwestern front, seesaw battles had cut a bloody swath through such fighting units as the French 5th Infantry.

For nine days and nine nights the French and British struggled to turn the flank of the German forces opposing them. Private Roget and his comrades had stormed the German defenses again and again. The Germans, well dug in, threw them back every time. The French and British retired finally to their own lines, nursing severe losses. They needed reinforcements desperately.

But the Germans had strengthened their own battle units first. They rushed in fresh troops, with heavy artillery and mortar support. Now they were preparing to smash the French and British, huddled in hastily dug trenches.

Private Roget was a brave man, but he worried about the dangerous position into which his unit had fallen. Until two months before this moment, life had been pleasant. He had worked in the warm country vineyards south of Toulouse. Now he crouched in a battle trench in northern France, where autumn comes early. With shells bursting about him, Roget pressed himself against the damp earth of his trench and wondered if he would still be alive at the end of the day.

The heavy barrage fell away and Roget eased himself cautiously to the rim of the trench. For a moment the war seemed far away. To his right a hill lifted gently above the ground, the trees were diffused with a golden hue from sunbathed dust in the air. It was a strange moment of peace.

Suddenly something moved within the woods. The movement at first startled him; then he relaxed. He knew that a strong body of British troops, including a full company of cyclist soldiers, was concealed in the woods. They, too, were waiting for reinforcements.

But there was movement *away* from the point where the British had dug in. The activity Private Roget saw was to the rear of the British position. Roget studied the area. There! He noticed it again. Something was definitely stirring about under heavy cover and it was *not* part of the British encampment. Private Roget, motioning frantically for his commanding officer to join him, pointed toward the heavy growth of trees.

The French officer brought powerful field glasses to his eyes. He scanned the area, then concentrated on a small break in the growth. After a moment he was able to make out a helmet. Several more moved into the range of his glasses. There was no longer any doubt. The helmets were worn by German troops who had somehow maneuvered to get behind the Allied lines, and were now waiting in ambush for the Allied reinforcements.

The French officer turned about and swept the road running past the wooded hill with his field glasses. In the valley below he saw the French relief column approaching the battlefield—two thousand soldiers marching behind their mounted officers into certain death.

Private Roget's officer pointed to the approaching column. "We must warn them!" he shouted to his men.

A signalman crawled from the trench. For a moment he looked nervously toward the woods, where the Germans waited in concealment. Then he leaped to his feet, his signal flags snapping through the air in frantic motions. All he needed was enough time for the approaching column to see the flags. Only a few more seconds . . .

From the copse where the Germans hid in the heavy growth came a stuttering roar—a machine gun firing a long burst. The signalman's body jerked violently, spun about. Dead before he struck the ground, the soldier tumbled back into the trench. Roget rushed to help him, then glanced at the officer and shook his head.

The French commander looked at the dismayed faces of his men. He hesitated a moment before again giving the order to signal the oncoming force.

A second signalman crouched, then rushed from the trench and scooped up the flags from the muddy ground. In an instant he stood erect, the semaphore flags moving quickly. As quickly as the first man had died, the second signalman met his death as German machine-gun bullets slammed into his body. He was hurled violently to the mud, his face a bright red flower.

The French officer rushed to his command post. Another way must be found to warn the reinforcing column of its danger. Yet to climb from the trenches was certain death. Abruptly, the assembled officers turned at a shout from Private Roget, who was gesturing toward the wooded hill.

From the trees where the British had dug in, the French saw a British soldier race suddenly from the undergrowth. He moved with uncommon speed and the French stared in wonder as the trooper tore down the hill on a bicycle, leaning sharply from one side to the other as he rode in zigzag spurts to confuse the aim of the German gunners.

Almost at once the Germans opened fire. The first burst went high. Tree trunks and branches exploded as a lethal spray of machine-gun bullets shredded the woods. The cyclist bent low, swerving sharply, pedaling even faster. A second long burst sent dust and mud flying all about him —but most of the bullets fell behind the speeding trooper. The Frenchmen began to cheer, but only for a moment. Their sudden shouting froze in their throats. The Germans had the range now. The heavy gun erupted with its deadly cough and bullets tore into the body of the British soldier.

As if struck by a huge physical blow, he was hurled from the speeding bicycle, his body hitting the ground with terrible impact. Blood poured from a dozen wounds as the dying man rolled through leaves and mud.

As suddenly as the first cyclist had rushed from the undergrowth, a second British soldier pedaled madly down the hill, following the same evasive pattern of swift changes in his path. Again the cheering rose from the trenches where the French watched, and again the heavy machine gun sought the range.

The second rider managed another fifty yards before the blast of lead caught him. Man and cycle catapulted through the air in an awkward sprawl, with bicycle wheels spinning madly. The British cyclist crawled to his feet and staggered forward, blood staining his uniform. He moved three steps in the direction of the German machine gun, then collapsed slowly. Lying down as if he were tired, he died on the spot.

Private Roget and his comrades gaped and shook their heads in wonder. Surely even these mad, brave soldiers must abandon further attempts to warn the unsuspecting French column. To expose oneself before that machine gun was suicide. The situation had become utterly hopeless. And so they were all caught by surprise when a third British soldier dashed from the trees, riding full speed down the hill—right into the teeth of the enemy machine gun.

Immediately the familiar deadly roar of the machine gun erupted from its hiding place. Again the bullets slashed the air and ripped through trees. But this time they failed to find their target. The cyclist raced on.

Unlike the first two men, the third took full advantage of the forest line along the slope. Head bent low, he raced his bicycle expertly between the trees, constantly changing position, offering a poor, fleeting target. The German gunner did his best to track his elusive quarry but could not keep pace with the agility and swiftness of the adroit cyclist. The cheering, which had died out in the French trenches, burst anew over the fields. Machine-gun bullets tore into trees, buzzing like hornets about the British soldier. Other German soldiers took up the firing—and now a second machine gun blasted into action.

In the valley below, the heavy fire had alerted the column of reinforcements. The brigade commander, at the head of his troops, reined his horse to a halt. The column stopped, alert for any danger. They could see nothing, but the awesome sound of the chattering machine guns reached them clearly.

Without warning, startling the French, the British cyclist exploded into sight. One moment nothing was there, the next second the French saw the soldier pedaling furiously from the shelter of the trees. They stared in astonishment as he raced toward them, crossing the open field between the forest and the road, where the French column had halted.

Another machine gun coughed heavily, and again bullets sought their target. The gunner stitched a straight line through thick grass. This time he had the range. Bullets slammed into the front wheel of the speeding bicycle!

But the cyclist was ready for this moment. He had already crossed the field to the road, and the instant he felt the wheel spokes cut by bullets, he lunged from the bicycle into the ditch.

The watching French troops fell silent. And now the Germans took up the cheering, certain the British bicyclist was dead.

But they couldn't see into the ditch. Hidden from view, the British trooper was a long way from being dead. Staying low he crawled along the ditch, dragging his bicycle with him. A hundred yards further along, convinced the Germans would never look for him there, he bounded from the ditch, climbed upon his bicycle, and rode with all speed toward the waiting French column.

Sudden shouts came from the German position. Men cursed and swung their heavy weapons about to take new aim. The machine guns roared again. But by this time the cyclist had made good his escape. He was beyond their range. Dirt spattered wildly along the road from falling bullets—all of them striking *behind* the speeding soldier.

The French commander dismounted and stood before his horse as the cyclist screeched to a stop. Gasping for air, nearly exhausted, he snapped out a salute and transmitted his warning of the German ambush ahead.

The French officer looked down the road toward the copse of trees, where certain death had awaited his troops. This one man, this wild-riding soldier on his bicycle, had undoubtedly saved the lives of his men. Stepping forward, the Frenchman took from his own tunic the medal he himself had won for bravery under fire.

"This medal was given to me, *mon camarade*, for saving one life," he said to the astonished Briton. Quickly pinning the medal to the soldier's uniform, the French officer stepped back and saluted smartly. "I have the honor," he declared, "of presenting it to you today for saving the lives of hundreds."

2

The First One Hundred and Five Years

There's something stirring and dramatic in the sight of men flying, sailing, or driving off to war.

But *pedaling?*

Well, it's far better than walking. Ask any foot slogger and you won't lack an answer.

Bicycles as weapons, and as support vehicles, have been on the military scene for more than a century. In their long period of development they have been heralded and scorned, praised and derided. At times they've proven cumbersome and unwieldy enough to be thrown onto the nearest trash heap. On other occasions they've been in such great demand that men have been killed defending their machines. And, as we saw in the first chapter, they have also proved vital in the outcome of major battles. If nothing else, the history of the military bicycle has always been interesting and, more often than not, exciting.

Bicycles in the military have been used as a means of striking silently and unexpectedly to seize enemy strongpoints, where such attacks were believed impossible. Special teams, as well as individuals, have used cycles to carry

10

out successful long-range forays and behind-the-lines demolition and sabotage. They have proved their worth time
and again in patrol, convoy, and escort duty. Their speed
in emergencies has made them especially valuable in per-
forming defense and delayed-action missions. Riot police
have testified to the merit of bicycles in controlling
crowds, moving swiftly over ground impassable to
other forms of transport. Bicycles have been unspindled,
folded, and racked into compact packages for paratroopers and mountain forces. In modern times, the lowly bicycle, sans the glitter of weaponry, has been at times virtually the sole logistics force of entire armies.

Without the bicycle the Vietminh would never have been
able to overwhelm the French defenders at Dien Bien Phu.
And without the bicycle in the hands of the Vietcong and
the North Vietnamese, the United States would have ended
the war in Vietnam years before it dragged to its unsuc-
cessful nonconclusion.

In Asia, more than in any other part of the world, the
bicycle survived against a massive assault by the most advanced and sophisticated weapons in history. It was the
simple bicycle that reigned supreme in jungle logistics,
and finally became, through its consistent success, one of
the most-sought-after targets along the supply trails of the
Vietnamese jungles.

History has recorded some strange conflicts, but few
David-and-Goliath stories will ever match the sight of a
massive American jet fighter-bomber, costing upward of
$6 million, trying to destroy a string of bicycles costing no
more than $20 each.

The bicycle had been around for a century before it
earned its greatest success in the wars that have plagued
Indochina in the last few decades. In the intervening hun-

dred years the military bicycle has seen many ups and downs in its development.

It all began during the Franco-Prussian War of 1870–1871. At that time, an enterprising tactician approached military officials of the French government with the proposition of using bicycles to conduct armed scouting expeditions in enemy territory.

What a surprise it would be! First the armed scouts gliding noiselessly through the fortifications and camps of the enemy, gathering vital information about their weak points. Then, the weaknesses well-recorded, task forces of specially trained soldiers racing deep into the enemy's land —to strike and disappear as silently and as mysteriously as they had come.

Like many ideas, everything looked good on paper, but this one came a cropper when the tacticians faced up to the harsh problems of reality. To begin with, the bicycles of 1870 were, by today's standards, crude in design, clumsy in use, distressingly heavy, and notoriously unreliable in their ability to survive in rough country.

Soldiers burdened with rifle, pack, and supplies needed acrobatic agility, great strength, and infinite patience simply to wobble their way along the cowpaths that served for roads in those days. More often than not, soldiers on foot, overtaking the "speedy cyclists," found them panting in total exhaustion in a ditch by the road. Initial experiments with the bicycle as a swift and silent weapon proved it to have all the bad characteristics of a mule with none of its advantages.

Well—no guts, no glory. The Italian army, studying the experiences of the French, responded with many a sneer at the "northerners." What could one expect from the

French? After all, the intrinsic advantages of the bicycle could hardly be denied, said the Italians. Without fuel or servicing, it promised far-ranging speed and mobility. One needed only to know how to improve the clumsy machines.

French bicycles were still rusting by the roadside, where they had been flung in disdain, when the Italian army put its theories into practice. In 1870, taking the best bicycles to be had on the open market, the Italians introduced the two-wheelers to their famed *bersaglieri*, the crack sharp-shooters of the army infantry corps. For five years grinning riflemen wheeled their cycles up and down the roads of Italy, waving to pretty girls—and pedaling off to meet those same girls under cover of darkness.

But would the machines that encouraged such clandestine meetings also function under the adversities of an army in the field? In 1875 the Italian army carried out large-scale maneuvers, duplicating battle conditions as closely as possible—and to everyone's surprise, especially that of the French, the bicycle came out a winner.

Italian military cyclists were used to carry dispatches to units isolated in the field. Notwithstanding the fact that even the best machines of that period were clumsy, heavy, and a nightmare of crude gearing, the cyclists averaged a speed of twelve miles an hour across open country. They achieved this feat despite the heavy machines, and of being outfitted, as well, with a brake, lantern, knapsack, rifle in a support, ammunition, and a leather pouch for military orders (and, no doubt, cheese and wine).

Reports of the bicycle's success in the Italian field maneuvers of 1875 sparked a rush by other countries to begin their own experimental programs. As inventors and tinkerers were turned loose, the bicycle showed up in a bewildering variety of designs and shapes. It grew in size and complexity as rapidly as the enthusiasm of its supporters could be translated into physical hardware.

Such progression is inevitable. The lure of "bigger and better" is irresistible. Thus the line of reasoning that if the bicycle, with its constant demand for balance on thin and hard tires, still had advantages over walking, what might not be done with the tricycle? So the three-wheeler was rushed from the factory to the army for field tests, and bore immediate fruit in reports that over good roads it could carry heavy loads with reasonable speed.

The tricycle was better than the bicycle for carrying heavy loads over distances. What might be the next step? You guessed it. The quadricycle lumbered away from the assembly shop, a contraption of machinery demanding the leg power and body stamina of two men. The concept itself could hardly be faulted. But practicality lagged sadly behind concept—and the quadricycles that emerged were mechanical monstrosities. Lumbering on thin tires, and with ungainly bodies desperately in need of spring action, they jolted and rocked wildly over the rutted and potholed roads in battle areas. However, despite their staggering faults, they proved even more dangerous to the enemy than to their riders—for there was nothing preposterous in the mounting of machine guns or other weapons on the quadricycles' bulky frames.

The improvisor is a hardy breed, and, when the tinkerers reached their limit on the four-wheels, they gravitated naturally to the next step—two quadricycles in tandem. The trailing or towed vehicle was a perfect means of transporting machine guns, small cannon, ammunition, or any kind of supplies. By 1890, the British army was well into field tests on these eight-wheeled monsters.

It didn't take long for them to become known as the "hernia horrors." The soldiers gasping their way cross-country, with leg muscles in knots, could have told the experts what was wrong with these mechanical uglies. Unless the road surface was of high quality, both men and machines took a beating that all too quickly put them out of action. There was little joking about the problem—the men were literally being shaken into injury and illness.

Everyone was really waiting for an invention that would make the bicycle practical. Solid tires had never been the answer and never would be. Something better was needed for rolling across the countryside. Unknown to those with battered bladders, that new invention had already been created by a horse doctor in Belfast, Ireland. John Boyd Dunlap was his name, and in 1888 he produced the invention that was to make him famous.

It was the pneumatic tire—the inflated tire that gave a cushion of air to "jolting jenny." Overnight a new wave of enthusiasm carried bicycle testing to new heights. The pneumatic tire was actually the turning point for the military bicycle, since it gave the machine unexcelled mobility over roads that had proved impassable for the earlier machines.

In 1892 the United States Army joined the parade of bicycle improvisors, beginning a series of extensive military field tests that offered fertile territory to the tinkerers. Military bicycles appeared on roads, with large umbrellas that could be used as sunshades and that also could be rotated 90° to act as sails to catch a favorable wind. Farmers gaped at these apparitions—two-wheeled sailing ships flitting over narrow country roads and gliding effortlessly over distant hills.

Unfortunately, that was the ideal. All too often the um-

brella-sails dragged their kicking riders into ditches and
off bridges into streams. They twisted and, more than
once, folded with a sudden *whack* across the heads of hapless riders. Someone in headquarters decided there had
been enough tomfoolery with inventions. It was time to
concentrate on using the bicycle as it had been designed—
for simple, reliable, and fast transportation.

The 15th Infantry was given the job of developing the
bicycle as a useful weapon. Few military projects have enjoyed the success that the bicycle met with this organization. A detachment of eight soldiers, under the command
of 1st Lt. W. T. May, spent several weeks becoming accustomed to their two-wheelers. They practiced loading with
rifles and supplies until they could mount up and be on
their way cross-country with only a few minutes' warning
—as soldiers, not sightseers.

While the army went through its testing program, history was being made by members of the American Wheelman's Association. Relays of bicycle carriers posted by the
AWA covered a distance of 975 miles in the amazing time
of only four days and thirteen hours, carrying a dispatch
from the Headquarters Department of the Missouri in
Chicago to the Headquarters Department of the East in
New York.

Another organization also had begun its own development program. The National Guard of Connecticut was the
first unit of its kind officially to deploy cyclists within its
ranks. This same guard outfit was actually the first American military organization to use the bicycle as standard
equipment assigned to its troops.

But the purists will argue that peacetime training just
isn't in the same league as roughing it in the field. It was
Maj. Gen. Nelson A. Miles (who had commanded army

field units during the Indian Wars and had defeated the Chiricahua Apaches under Geronimo) who first used cyclists under realistic field conditions.

Working under special handicaps of mountain country, Miles organized the 25th Infantry Bicycle Corps in July 1896 at Fort Missoula, Montana. Second Lieutenant James A. Moss was assigned as commander. Moss not only was the first man to command a cycle corps, he was the only white man in the outfit, which was all-Negro in its ranks.

They were also a brilliant team. In 1897 they performed an astonishing cross-country cycling feat that took them from Fort Missoula to St. Louis, Missouri, in thirty-four days.

There were many tests other than racing cross-country. In 1896, Capt. R. E. Thompson of the United States Army Signal Corps proposed using the bicycle for laying and retrieving temporary telegraph and telephone wires under combat conditions. He invented a special device, to be attached to a bicycle, that could run a length of wire over a distance of 1,800 yards, and could reel it back, within two minutes. Thompson received authorization to test his invention in the field.

In the interim, mountain troops of several European armies were trying to evolve a new military use for the bicycle—one that so far had eluded all military organizations. Much of Europe consists of steep and mountainous country, often plagued with sucking mud and laced with impassable terrain, as well as countrysides abounding in walls and fences. Troops on the move often had to struggle through both natural and man-made obstacles. If there was any hope for the bicycle as a means of individual transport, it must be able to go where the soldier went—when he was walking or climbing. Austrian and French in-

ventors introduced machines that could be folded easily
and secured to a pack, to be carried on the back of a soldier when he had to leave the road. The first folding bicycles weighed about twenty-eight pounds.

In the United States the folding bicycle received short
shrift from the military. Ignoring the built-in problems of
sliding and folding parts, Maj. R. P. Davidson of Northwestern Military Academy at Lake Geneva, Wisconsin,
launched his own development program. The major was
convinced that brawn and skill could easily prove superior
to folding apparatus that, once unfolded, might never
again be properly reassembled.

Davidson organized sixteen cadets into a bicycle corps.
Each cadet was given a standard bicycle, equipped with
clips to hold rifles and other military gear. Davidson
wasn't content simply to have his cadets race along roads.
He wanted them to be able to go virtually anywhere, and
his cadets soon discovered the major meant what he said.
They practiced slinging the cycles onto their backs and
fording streams. They climbed hills and clambered along
gullies. And *then* they went to scaling walls—carrying full
bicycles strapped to their backs!

The first attempts to clamber over walls, each man en-
cumbered by the weight and clumsy mass of his bicycle,
produced a rash of skinned knees, elbows, and bleeding
fingers. Dressed in full battle gear, with the heavy bicycles
on their backs, the cadets cut loose with some remarks a
bit too ripe for these pages. Davidson permitted no slack
as he hammered at his charges. Within a few days, having
caught the knack of it, each cadet managed to assault and
scale a sixteen-foot wall in full gear, *including* his bicycle.
Once they knew it could be done, they redoubled their
efforts. Within a week they were functioning as a smooth

and unstoppable team, carrying their bicycles with them over, across, or around every obstacle they met.

Major Davidson, initially the laughingstock of the army with his program, reaped his full reward when he was recognized for his leadership and was told his efforts with his cadets had led directly to a new program of military bicycle development.

Before the year was out the army had commissioned the Pope Manufacturing Company to produce a bicycle on which a Colt automatic machine gun was to be mounted. The machine-gun cycle proved surprisingly effective in field maneuvers, and soon Pope was hard at work on a tandem bicycle that was a rolling fortress—bristling with a 12-shot repeating rifle, two Colt quick-action revolvers, a case of signal flags, ammunition, two rolled overcoats, and two rolled blankets.

Again the specter of runaway innovation reared its mechanical head. Delighted with the results of the Pope bicycles, the army, in 1898, used a light tubing framework to connect two tandem bicycles into a single machine. Across the connecting tubes they placed a detachable stretcher of light steel tubing, with handles made from handlebar grips. Thus the bicycle ambulance was born.

On February 15, 1898, the battleship U.S.S. *Maine* went to the bottom of Havana harbor, after a violent explosion that claimed the lives of 266 men aboard. Five weeks later demolition experts reported that the *Maine* had been the victim of a mine placed deliberately against the hull, and one month later the United States declared war against Spain. Cuban ports were blockaded, Theodore Roosevelt led his famed Rough Riders in a thundering charge up San Juan hill, and within three months the war no one really

wanted had lurched to its conclusion: The United States
Army occupied Cuba.

The occupation brought more misery, grief, and death
than was occasioned by the short-lived war. Without necessary preparations for bivouac in the tropics, especially during the wet summer season, yellow fever and malaria
swept through both military and civilian ranks. As the
Cubans fell victim by the thousands, they reacted with
mob violence. Riots turned the streets into shambles.
Stricken United States soldiers were removed from the island, and a call went out for Maj. Gen. Nelson A. Miles to
send in troops for riot-control duty.

Lt. James A. Moss and the black troops of the 25th Infantry Bicycle Corps had their chance. They sailed at once
for Cuba and went immediately on riot-control duty, using
their bicycles in loose formation to patrol the troubled
city of Havana. The complete story of the corps' operations
in Cuba is told later on in this narrative, but it is sufficient
to say now that there have been few times when the military bicycle was better proven as an instrument for preventing violence.

War is one of man's more active pursuits, and within a
year of the Spanish-American War a new conflict erupted
across the plains of South Africa. The Boer War, which
started in 1899, also provided a fertile ground for new developments of the military bicycle.

The key was modifying the standard assembly of the bicycle, and the new hero of the day was an English manufacturer, Dursley Pedersen, whose folding bicycle was a
vast improvement over the bulky machines with which
most soldiers had been burdened.

The compact shape of the folded bicycle and its light

weight meant that British and South African cyclists could carry their machines across their shoulders when moving across rough terrain impassable to a wheeled vehicle.

The success of the Pedersen bicycle in the Boer War galvanized other countries to conduct renewed tests. Within a year, France, Germany, Italy, Belgium, Russia, Switzerland, and Japan had adopted the folding bicycle as standard military equipment. Innovation had given way to steady, reliable improvement, and bicycle brigades became an integral element in most armed forces.

By the time the Great War flamed across Europe in 1914, folding bicycles were as common as other transport or weapons. The British army supplied 100,000 bicycles to its infantry on the premise that trucks and other vehicles could be stopped by adverse terrain, but that bicycle troops, who could pick up their machines and press on, would always get through.

It was a procedure followed by other armies, and when the great battles raged across Europe, bicycle troops were often in the spearhead of clashing forces. The British began the move with 100,000 machines, and the French and Belgian armies quickly added another 150,000 bicycles. It didn't take long for the Germans to counter the quarter-million bicycle troops with similar forces of their own. Throughout the early operations in the Ardennes, French observers often called for immediate pursuit and destruction of German cyclists on reconnaissance and security missions.

By the time the United States entered the war with the first troops of the American Expeditionary Force, hundreds of thousands of bicycles were in use along the front. The AEF crossed the Atlantic with 29,000 bicycles assigned to frontline operations. Unlike the European forces, however, the United States Army lacked a specifically designated bicycle corps, and its two-wheelers were used for communication, unit reconnaissance, recreation, and as a means of supplementary transport.

Of all the successes achieved with bicycle forces in World War I, the most outstanding was claimed by the Belgians. In late September 1914, a Belgian commander— who had a special fondness for striking at German communications lines—organized a commandolike force of seven volunteer cyclist detachments. Each detachment was made up of two officers and about 100 enlisted men. A small demolitions team filled out the individual force.

During the two-week period between September 25 and October 9, 1914, the Belgian bicycle commandos launched five major raids behind German lines. Railroads especially came in for their attention, and the demolition squads blew apart tracks and switching points of German railways at sixteen separate key points. Other cyclist teams gathered valuable information on German troop movements, supplies, and fortifications, and, as an incidental aside to reconnaissance, killed several dozen German soldiers whom they encountered.

Only one bicycle commando team suffered heavy losses. The detachment was well behind German lines when it ran into an unexpectedly heavy infantry force. In the raging fight that broke out, sixty Belgians were killed—but not before they inflicted heavy casualties on the Germans, and succeeded in blowing up both ends of a key tunnel on the rail line between Brussels and Mons.

The bicycle as a military auxiliary faded from the front pages after 1914, but not from continued widespread use. In the summer of 1917, an entire German cyclist brigade was transferred to the eastern front to augment the force

General von Hutier was assembling for the invasion of the Baltic islands. In this unusual and carefully planned operation, two complete German cyclist battalions participated in the initial assault against Oesel Island, and distinguished themselves in the capture of that island, where a high degree of mobility was essential.

One of the most noted military leaders of World War I— Gen. von Lettow Vorbeck, the German commander in East Africa—paid special tribute to the effectiveness of the bicycle as a key element in his operations. Vorbeck had been equipped with only a few motorized vehicles in East Africa, and when these wore out or were destroyed the entire military staff was left without transport—except for the bicycle. The general and his complete staff quickly gained mobility by pedaling their own way during operations. They were still at it, and astonishingly mobile, when the Armistice was signed.

Certain people, who were interested in military strife after World War I came to its final, bloodied halt, had taken special note of the effectiveness of the bicycle in some forms of military operations. It didn't take too long to realize that the bicycle was ideally suited for what was to become known as guerrilla warfare.

The booming echoes of a world war were still being heard when Ireland renewed its bitter internal struggles, and a group known as the Irish Volunteers launched a guerrilla war campaign against armed police and military forces. Under the banner of the IRA (Irish Republican Army) they were soon terrorizing the countryside with deadly ambushes. The bushwhacking tactics graduated to full-scale assaults against troop barracks and convoys.

Violence invariably begets violence and the government

retaliated in kind. Swiftly and bloodily, Ireland was po-
litically sundered. When a large number of the Irish police
threw off their uniforms, they were replaced swiftly with
recruits from England, who became known as the Black-
and-Tans because of the color of their uniforms. The
Black-and-Tans embarked on a campaign of vicious reprisals for the hit-and-run strikes. Violence flared to the extent that the Black-and-Tans set fire to a large section of
Cork when it seemed that reprisals were the only way to
deal with the continued uprising.

Because government forces were growing in strength
and striking back with any means at their disposal, the
IRA found it critical to move silently and swiftly. And for
the purposes of guerrilla conflict, especially in rough country, there was no better machine than the bicycle.

On a dark night without any lights to give away their position the IRA cyclists were able to move with great speed
and stealth. Hidden by the cloak of darkness they sabo-
taged communications lines, destroyed bridges, cut railways, and struck with telling effect against police and military centers. The government authorities never knew when
shadowy forms would emerge from the cover of darkness,
shatter the quiet gloom with flaming explosions or bursts
of gunfire, and then disappear on their bicycles without a
sound.

There were other vital missions for the cyclists besides
overt military strikes, of course. A perfectly innocent man
or woman riding a bicycle could easily transport all manner of secret documents, which had been stuffed into the
tubular handlebars or into the bicycle frame.

All smuggling didn't take place at night, for the guerrillas were bold and brazen. There's the famous story in Ireland of the shapely lass who rode her bicycle frequently

down heavily guarded roads, nodding and smiling at delighted guards. She became so well-known that passing nods blossomed into open recognition, and soon the "friendships" were so many that the guards would often wave her through their checkpoints and barricades without any inspection or question.

Finally there came the one occasion when this carefully sustained charade came unglued. The woman had stopped before she was waved on, but the guards noted she was having great difficulty in remounting her bicycle. Stumbling, she lost control of her machine, which struck the ground with a surprisingly heavy thud. One of the friendly guards hurried to her aid.

We can imagine the shock on his face when he found it impossible to lift the bicycle from where it lay on the ground. Other guards came up and surprise turned at once to suspicion. They opened the tubular steel sections of the bicycle—and found them lined solidly with gold that had been melted down and poured into them. Swiftly friendship flew out the nearest window and they turned to sieze the girl. The shapely lass, however, had already vanished from the scene.

The bicycle, as used by the IRA, so bedeviled the English —and its success was so widespread—that army leaders throughout Europe renewed their interest in developing special-purpose forces that could put the bicycle to greater military advantage.

Aiding this new concentration on the bicycle was a series of factors: first, there was the extensive experience and success of bicycles as used by the IRA; second, bicycles had improved greatly in design. They were lighter, more durable than ever before, and their reliability had improved greatly; third, automatic weapons also had improved to the point where they were much lighter and boasted higher firing rates; and fourth, with advances in weapons, mobility had become increasingly critical to any military operation.

Thus the new demands emerged. The well-trained and well-equipped soldier on a bicycle was a more dangerous and effective fighting man than the same soldier on foot.

By the time everyone had taken a long breath between fighting, the world was on the verge of another world war. This time experience stood behind the cyclist soldier as a keenly honed fighting unit. He appeared in special brigades to rush to the scene of conflict with machine guns and grenade-firing rifles. He was a dangerous force in silent wars of sabotage. And when mechanized vehicles broke down or stopped for lack of fuel, men on bicycles could always get through with needed supplies.

What worked in Europe was just as meaningful elsewhere, of course. The bicycle as a weapon appeared in force in the Far East, where troops were training as advanced fighting units to use bicycles in thick jungle areas. Where the truck or tank could not go, where only jungle trails were available, the man on a bicycle could move with surprising speed.

And, for the first time, the bicycle soldier had the ability to leap oceans, rivers, plains, and mountains—in the form of the paratrooper who jumped from his plane with a folded bicycle secured to his back.

By the time World War II was getting into full swing the soldier bicyclist was an accepted and major force in European and Asian armies. But not in the United States. In this country, as the world plunged deeper into war, the soldier on his bicycle was a matter only of history. No plans existed for cyclist troops. The mechanized vehicle reigned supreme in military thinking. Troops would be moved by sea, they would roll on trucks and trains, they would fly—and when they reached their destinations, they would walk.

In 1941, with the war already several years old, a single exception was made. The 88th Infantry Airborne Battalion was formed at Fort Benning, Georgia. Five hundred men made up the battalion, and it was equipped with 280 bicycles, 140 motorcycles and a small number of jeeps.

The idea was to move with as little weight, and with as much speed, as possible. The troops were trained to parachute from their transport aircraft with bicycles secured to their backs. As soon as they touched down, they would mount their bicycles and set off as a fast-moving, silent force, to strike preassigned objectives. But the battalion never got further than the red clay hills of Georgia. The outfit sat out the entire war without foreign assignment.

Not so the soldier and guerrilla forces in other parts of the world. Sabotage and espionage teams were dropped in large numbers behind enemy lines—complete with folding bicycles. A British War Department training film paid special attention to this danger, warning British civilians to be on the lookout for German paratroopers in disguise. One scene dramatized the danger by showing a nun walking sedately on a quiet city street. Suddenly, the nun—who turns out to be a German soldier in disguise—slips a folding bicycle from beneath "her" habit, assembles it, and rides off!

But while German cyclists were a daily fear in England, in France, and in Belgium, it was the Germans who came to hate the bicycle most. Acts of sabotage carried out by individuals or by special striking teams became so widespread that just to be riding a bicycle at certain times of day, or in sensitive areas, was cause for suspicion and intensive questioning. Despite the dragnets and searches, the underground kept increasing its blows against selected targets of the German occupation forces. On May 8, 1942, alarmed by the worsening situation, the German command in Paris forbade the use of bicycles after dark in almost half of France.

What had burgeoned in France was sweeping like a prairie fire through Belgium. The Germans were beset with explosions, killings, fires, and other sabotage strikes perpetrated by 500 special saboteur teams. Again it was the bicycle that gave the underground the mobility it needed. So effective were these teams, using the bicycle to glide silently at night through city and countryside, that the underground forces were credited with being the key factor in preventing the Germans from destroying the vital port of Antwerp.

Yet of all the nations that made effective use of the bicycle as a primary military weapon, none matched the expertise of the Japanese during their invasion of Malaya and during the fall of Singapore in 1942. The Japanese, more than any other military group, fully appreciated the ability of the bicycle-riding soldier to move at a rapid and steady pace where no motorized vehicle could travel. Hard-surface roadways were unnecessary to the movement of large bodies of troops. If the Japanese soldier had a path no more than eighteen inches in width through the jungle, he would move steadily and swiftly to his target area. A Japanese leader who understood this factor, and put it to excellent use, was Gen. Tomoyuki Yamashita, who became famous as the "Tiger of Malaya." His clever use of the bicycle, of innovative scare tactics, and his skill in doing what the British least expected him to do were largely influential in the Japanese takeover of Malaya and Singapore.

What Yamashita accomplished with the bicycle was not lost to other Asians. In French Indochina, which the Japanese had occupied with little or no resistance before their main assaults after December 7, 1941, the insurgent guerrilla forces of Ho Chi Minh, led by Gen. va Nguyen Giap, waited out the war. One day the Japanese would be defeated. When that day came, the guerrillas would be ready to assert themselves.

It didn't work out that way. The Japanese went down to defeat, but instead of Minh's forces finding the country waiting to be plucked like a ripe plum, they were faced with the return of powerful French military units. When the French reoccupied Indochina, the guerrilla leaders decided they had no choice but to fight for their land.

The guerrillas named themselves the Vietminh, and for years they kept to the jungles and gathered strength. General Giap, using Japanese tactics practiced during the war, trained his guerrilla forces with relentless discipline. By 1950 he judged his jungle soldiers ready to take on the French and start the battle to oust them from the country.

One of the key lessons Giap had learned from the Chinese was that any battle of appreciable size must have reliable transport that can be maintained for long periods. Giap turned now to the legacy of Gen. Tomoyuki Yamashita and built up a complex system of porters who could move vast quantities of food and ammunition by bicycle. Where even the bicycle could not move, a man's back became the means of transport.

Giap developed bicycle transport for combat supply to its finest art. By adding wooden struts to strengthen the frame and the front fork of Peugeot bicycles, and by using bamboo poles to extend one handlebar and the brake levers, Giap created a machine that could haul 500 pounds of supplies.

This was ten to twelve times the load that could be carried by a man on foot, and more than an elephant could haul through jungle terrain.

Giap had prepared his army well by the time he was ready for his showdown with the French at their powerful fortress of Dien Bien Phu. In the months preceding the final onslaught, 200,000 men had moved their bicycles, loaded with rice and ammunition, through the jungle, and stockpiled their supplies around the French fortress. The French, of course, did everything possible to destroy the primitive transport system, but not even massive air attacks with napalm could do more than slightly delay the determined bicycle-supply effort.

In March 1954 the Vietminh began closing in for the kill, in early May Dien Bien Phu fell, and a month later the French government yielded its position in Indochina, with the guerrilla force controlling Vietnam north of the Ben-Hoi River, at the 17th Parallel.

On July 21, at a conference in Geneva, an armistice went into effect. The communists set up the Democratic Republic of Vietnam, with the capital at Hanoi. Ho Chi Minh became president. With political promises for a time of peace and plenty, the people of Indochina looked forward to better times in both South and North Vietnam.

It didn't take long for their hopes to be shattered. Infiltrators from the north worked their way into the small communities of South Vietnam to recruit sympathizers for the communist cause. Those who volunteered or were selected were then trained in terrorist and guerrilla warfare, and organized under the banner of the National Front of Liberation of South Vietnam—better known as the Vietcong.

Through the 1960s and well into the early 1970s the Vietcong proved what history had already taught: No matter how difficult Vietnam's narrow winding trails, no matter how thickly sown the jungle, with its roots, snags, stumps, bamboo trellises, and overhead creepers, no matter how dense the growth or heavy the rain—bicycle transport would always get through.

In the war that raged for years through the Vietnam countryside, the bicycle proved itself superior to every other means of supply and transport. Not even the most concentrated and modern airpower and electronic systems could stem the tributaries of supply in the jungle. Since the bicycle moved with almost complete silence, the soldier porters almost always had time to melt away from open trails and to hide in dense growth. It was a frustrating and ineffective way to fight a war—pitting multimillion-dollar jet fighter-bombers against the hundreds of twisting, brush-choked trails that snaked their way across mountains and through jungles. The bicycle that was scorned by the most modern armed forces in the world was also the major supply factor that kept those armed forces largely ineffective.

To support the savage fighting throughout South Vietnam, where the Vietcong battled the South Vietnamese army and the vast force of the United States, the North Vietnamese poured down the Ho Chi Minh Trail, with thousands of porters riding bicycles loaded with food, supplies, and ammunition. No matter what steps were used to stem the flow it was never effective—and the history of the final outcome in Vietnam is no older than yesterday's newspapers.

3

The Oddballs

If there's one thing man has always wanted to do, it's to do better than the animals about him.

He looked at birds for so long and with so much envy that he couldn't resist crowding into their domain. After all, if a bird could fly, why not a man? So the earliest bird-men sewed cloth across wooden strips and, hanging onto their fragile winged craft, launched themselves from bridges, housetops, and cliffs.

And promptly fell straight down to bust their—ah, necks.

There were men who envied and did their best to emulate creatures in the sea. Of course, if man couldn't obtain oxygen from sea water as did fish and seagoing mammals, at least he was smart enough to build an airtight undersea vessel, and carry his oxygen along with him. Right? It shows how to do it, right there on those drawings.

And as fast as inventors built their new-fangled submarines they invented new ways to get to the bottom of the sea, where they either tried frantically to get back to the surface or they drowned.

The point is that as men did their best to extend man's

own physical capabilities, they had something to use for an example.

Until someone came up with the idea of the bicycle. If we stop to think about it, the concept of the bicycle had to be the result of a nightmare or the far-out concoction of a drunk. Man wanted to fly because birds fly. He wanted to swim because fish and other mammals swim atop and beneath the water. He wanted to sail because the effects of wind upon large surfaces are glaringly evident.

But the *bicycle?* There isn't a thing in nature that is totally unbalanced while at rest, and gets its balance from the principle of gyroscopic motion—which can't be seen, felt, smelled, or whatever.

One suspects, then, that the man who invented the bicycle must have been a lunatic genius. Most inventors are either crazy or presumed to be crazy, and it's safe to assume that a Frenchman named Sirvac had to be at the head of the list of this fraternity. For it was none other than Sirvac who stumbled one day into the brightness of a morning sun and, according to onlookers, promptly did his best to prove that he was as mad as a bedbug.

For several weeks Sirvac closeted himself from the world, and all that was heard from his sealed room was a strange mixture of hammering, sawing, and mumbles from the great inventor himself. Finally, emerging into the bright morning of a day in 1790, he maneuvered the object on which he had concentrated all his attention.

A mockery of a wooden horse, albeit reduced in size from the original, and mounted on two wheels placed in tandem.

Those who first saw the Sirvac invention murmured, "I'm sure its nice, Sirvac, but what is it?"

Demonstration is often the best retort to questions like that, and Sirvac lost no time in proving the wonder he had created. Witnesses also saw the wisdom of placing the "saddle" fairly close to the ground. Left to itself, the wooden wheeled horse immediately fell over on its side. With Sirvac on the seat, his legs provided stability when at rest or moving slowly. Sirvac had judged that as soon as he got up some speed there would be an inherent balance to his contraption, and he would be coasting. If he went downhill, then the coasting promised to be something of a whiz-bang ride.

With commendable temerity he put his apparatus to the test. He gripped the wooden head with both hands and then propelled himself forward with alternate kicks of his feet against the ground. Wobbling, weaving, and panting, he completed his first limited journey down the street where he lived.

Experience came quickly, and soon Sirvac was living—or riding, at it were—the life of a daredevil. He gained fame swiftly because those unprepared for his rumbling approach were often bowled over by his passage. The more speed Sirvac gained, the louder he needed to shout warnings of his approach. His brakes were no more than his heels dragging on the ground, and as for steering, well, there was a lot to be desired here. The only way Sirvac could steer was by leaning from one side to the other—a dangerous procedure on his clumsy vehicle—or by smashing his fists on the side of the head of his wooden-horse-cycle in order to turn it from its path.

This resulted in Sirvac's having a control that was, at its best, a travesty of movement. As a result, he achieved a remarkable score in pedestrians knocked from their feet. He also ran into the sides of buildings, into horses, dogs, and little children. He collected an extraordinary range of

bruises upon his own person. Even if a ride proved successful in avoiding objects in his way, Sirvac was often seen
returning home whimpering and holding his bruised fists
carefully, because of the damage sustained in trying to
steer his self-made monster.

Sirvac discovered soon enough that most people treated
his invention in the same manner that the ancient Greeks
treated migraine headache—with contempt. This attitude
also assured that Sirvac would slip into history with an
obscurity sought by few inventors. Not for twenty-eight
years did someone ponder over the wooden thing Sirvac
had created, and ponder long enough to judge that, if
major improvements were made in the original idea, a
workable device might emerge from the effort.

In the year 1818, Baron Drais of Baden began the first of
the many improvements to come. If one rides a horse, he
reasoned, one can steer the beast by bringing him to turn
his head to the left or the right. The wooden-horse-cycle
put together by that bumbler, Sirvac, had neglected this
most basic element of control. So the good Baron placed
the front wheel of the vehicle on a vertical pivot, and added
a control lever that permitted the rider to guide himself.
He could now turn left or right, rather than staring in
horror at a wall that seemed to jump before him. There
were still no brakes, of course, and a rough surface meant
getting shaken, as though rolling over a high waterfall in a
barrel, but progress was being made.

No sooner had Baron Drais completed his significant
change in what was to become the bicycle than an unknown
inventor in England stepped into the act. Even a scaled-
down body of a horse made of wood was, he reasoned, a
monstrosity, and so he substituted an iron frame for the

timbered flanks created by Sirvac. For the first time, the bicycle was taking a shape we would, in later years, be able to recognize.

Thirty-seven years passed before another significant change was made. Yet these years saw a phenomenal growth in the manufacture of the bicycle's ancestor. If nothing else, the machine was now steerable, and plenty of people were ready to take a daring whirl at racing down slopes while the wind rushed past them.

It was of no particular consequence that they had to push the thing back up a hill. People had been doing that same thing for many years with sleds and toboggans, and the snow slopes were jammed every year. The same reasoning applies to skiers. If there's enough of a thrill in going down, there are plenty of people willing to work their way up. Besides, if the ground was reasonably level, it was still possible to move along by lustily kicking one's heels into the ground in erratic self-propulsion. Hardy barefoot boys found no problem in this means of locomotion, and cobblers encouraged those with shoes to take up the sport, since they often returned from their outings with leather soles and heels looking as though they'd been chewed by a small hungry bear.

By 1855 the time was ripe for the next major improvement—and it was in France, once again, that the genius of invention arose. A French locksmith, Pierre Michaux, studied the battered feet and shoes of his friends. Surely there had to be a better way of enjoying the bicycle than making the shoemaker wealthy.

Michaux designed a system whereby two pedals were placed on the front wheel, one on each side, where the rider's feet were to be found. This permitted the rider to propel the machine with footpower applied directly to the pedals rather than thumping shoes against the ground. The small horizontal bars extending from the steering pivot were considered by Michaux to be much too small for comfort or for proper steering control, so he refined this part of the machine by creating a T-shaped bar with horizontally extended branches—eventually to become the handlebars.

The machine was evolving. It now had free-moving wheels, footpedals for power, a vertical pivot for steering, and horizontal extensions for handlebars. It was becoming the bicycle in real truth. Known in those times as the velocipede, bearing the manufacturer's name of Michaux, it went into limited production as a device for pleasure. Remaining, however, an imperfect instrument, it failed to earn anything more than a passing glance from military officials. That time had to wait for further design improvements.

Again the French led the way, this time in the person of Surnay, who was adept with the use of ball bearings. Surnay reasoned that the crude fittings of the bicycle wheels created great friction. Friction meant drag, and drag meant inefficiency. Much of the energy, either from pedaling or from gravity, thus went into the production of heat rather than movement. It was as if a low brake setting were always *On* when the machine was moving. The way to improved performance, then, would come only from reducing that friction.

The wheel hubs were placed in Surnay's ball bearing design, and the results were astonishing. It was one thing to achieve high speed downhill in a bicycle without the bearings, but the effort over level ground or along a slight upgrade was enormous, and bicycle pathways were often littered with gasping and wheezing sportsmen. The ball bearings changed all that, and, soon after a number of the

Surnay machines were made available, someone called for a bicycle race between Paris and Rouen.

Now the bicycle caught the eye of the military, for the Paris–Rouen contest achieved an average speed for the full distance of nine miles an hour. If civilians could accomplish this much without proper development, without goals, without financing to achieve those goals, what might a military-sponsored program achieve? In 1870 the Franco-Prussian war provoked another of the frequent mass joustings on the European continent, and with the new spree of bloodletting came military experiments with the still-clumsy and still-archaic bicycle.

There is an old saying that necessity is the mother of invention—and no one ever needs things faster than an army in wartime—even the Italian army, which introduced the bicycle to its bersaglieri rifle battalions. Five years later, the soldiers had built up enormous leg muscles. They had improved the speed of cross-country pedaling from nine to twelve miles an hour. Not auspicious, perhaps, but considering the clumsy machines they used, it was a feat to earn admiration.

In 1870, production of the velocipede, as the bicycle was called in those times, had spread to a dozen or more factories. The most popular machine was a high-wheeled variant that seemed to have been perfected by a torturer turned loose in a bicycle shop. The machines were known as "boneshakers." Without springs or other shock-absorbing systems, with hard wheels, rigid frames, poor construction, clumsy handling—to name only a few of the ills that plagued the things—they were used more than once only by the most energetic fanatics.

Understand, then, the reaction of the frontline soldier when he learned of the program under way that required

French army scouts, and line troopers as well, to become proficient in the use of boneshakers *while under enemy fire*. Notwithstanding the horror that greeted arrival of the machines at the front, the soldiers were rushed into the range of German guns.

The Germans, after they had wiped the tears of laughter from their eyes, shot to ribbons any French unfortunate within their sights, and French soldier cyclists scurried for their lives as they abandoned their clumsy high-wheelers in ditches and behind concealing brush.

It was a strange twist of fate that brought the bicycle from France to England, with a promise of great improvement. Rowley Turner was an Englishman who had escaped the siege of Paris through his skill and stamina on one of the old boneshaker high-wheeling cycles. Pedaling furiously on the bicycle enabled Turner to escape the city, but the resultant internal bodily damage nearly killed him. Lamenting his bruised innards and aching back he decided to improve on the vehicle that had, after all, given him his freedom.

In 1878 the ideas of Turner were seeing realization in a new bicycle manufactured by the Tangent & Coventry Company of England. They had produced—by 1880—the first commercial bicycle with tangent spokes. Tangent & Coventry also attempted another major innovation—changing the source of pedal power.

Until this time the front wheel—the oversize high wheel —of the bicycle received the footpower of its rider. The wheel was so high that the machine was more of a monstrosity than a practical vehicle, and to mount his mechanical steed the cyclist needed to climb a ladder so that he would be high enough to swing onto the saddle. The saddle, or seat, was placed directly over the high wheel, while the rear wheel was so diminutive in size as to look like something left over and hurriedly bolted on.

Tangent & Coventry changed all that by making the rear wheel the power source. It was a move in the right direction, but it didn't go far enough. The company failed to alter the dimensions of the two wheels, and the cyclist still had to be a mixture of acrobat and weight lifter to emerge without bodily injury from any prolonged riding.

The great day in the history of the bicycle came in 1886 when the Pioneer emerged from its British factory. All of a sudden, it seemed, inventors were acquiring the skill so long and desperately needed in the development of the bicycle. The Pioneer was the direct predecessor to the machine we know today. Since the rear wheel was now the power source, it was increased in size. The seat was moved to a position almost midway between the wheels, and a chain-and-sprocket system was installed for transferring pedalpower to the rear wheel. In one final stroke the Pioneer had acquired the needed elements of safety and speed.

Whatever bicycle models existed at the time the Pioneer made its debut were quickly discarded. Improvements of all sorts cropped up in one new model after another. Ball bearing systems were introduced to the foot pedals. Handlebars were properly weighted and carefully sized for different riders. Angled and graceful frames replaced the original clumsy upright iron bodies. Spring saddles offered increased comfort.

In 1888 the Scots veterinarian, John Boyd Dunlop, entered the scene with the hollow pneumatic tire, and brought about another quantum jump in bicycle performance. Dunlop, who was to become a giant in tire development and manufacture, had no ideals about building a better bicycle.

The Belfast doctor had had enough of complaints from his son, whose tricycle jolted him to the point of bruises and tears. Dunlop studied the boy's machine, then formed a hollow tube from horse bandages, sealed off the tube except for a valve, and pumped the thing full of air. The pneumatic tire was born.

Militarists applied every new development to the war bicycle. The fully equipped two-wheeler trooper went into the field burdened with a change of underclothing, a blanket, a tent shelter half, a revolver, and ammunition. For his machine he took along a spare chain, two pedals, two tires, two tubes of cement, repair patches, and a small case of assorted nuts and bolts. Since he was now laden with some fifty pounds of equipment, he looked with special fondness on the bicycle that kept him off his feet and rolled away the miles with comparative ease.

One after the other, the military modifications came upon the scene. Bicycles with automatic machine guns and repeating rifles were joined with men carrying boxes of signal flags for communication across battlefields. The tricycle and the quadricycle, the infamous hernia horrors, appeared to bedevil soldiers. The umbrella sail came and went.

James C. Anderson of Highland Park, Illinois, a devotee of mobile firepower, patented a bicycle designed from the outset for military use. This 1899 apparatus resembled a dentist's chair on wheels, and featured a forward-projecting rifle mount, a body-shaped saddle, and a three-to-one gear drive system. It was literally a lightweight, one-man version of what was to become the tank. Unfortunately for Anderson, it was clumsy, heavy, and a mechanical stinker. The army showed Anderson the nearest door.

Tests and experiments are interesting, but too often they're also far from able to pass the acid test of operating under field conditions. It remained for the 25th Infantry Bicycle Corps, stationed at Fort Missoula, Montana—and an astonishing 1,900-mile trek—to bring true significance to the role of the military bicycle.

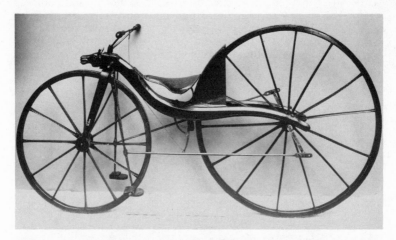

One of the more advanced "historical items" is this Macmillan model of 1839. Note the heavy wooden frame, nonsteering handbar, horse-head model, and the long "transmission drive" from the footpedals to the rear wheel. (*Montagu Motor Museum*)

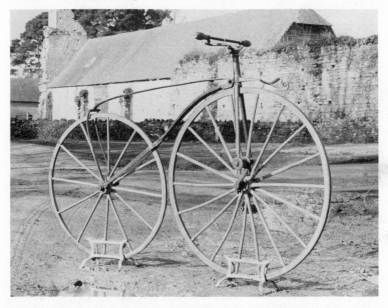

An original "boneshaker" of the 1865 period, complete with direct footpower drive to the front wheel. All wood and metal and no springs or "give," but at least the front wheel turned. (*Montagu Motor Museum*)

One of those days when the inventors should have stayed in bed, but didn't—and came up with this monocycle monstrosity. The idea was to stuff a soldier inside and send him hurtling at the enemy. Greene & Dyer of Providence, Rhode Island, turned out the lumbering disaster in 1869. Soldiers who tested the mono were often battered after losing control on hills. (*Smithsonian Institution*)

Humber's Tandem of 1896 vintage was an advanced model, with rubber tires, spring seats, modern handlebar, and chain drive. A number of the Humber Tandems, with a cargo box replacing the rear seat, became cargo carriers with the British army in the Boer War. (*Montagu Motor Museum*)

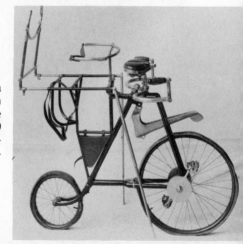

The Anderson military bicycle was a direct-drive rolling dentist's chair with special brackets for carrying machine guns, rifles, and supplies. It was the 1899 brainchild of James C. Anderson of Highland Park, Illinois. (*Smithsonian Institution*)

A Colt machine gun as it was fitted to an Army bicycle. The weapon weighed about forty pounds and presented serious balance problems to the rider. (*Dr. William E. Bagwell*)

Hillman, Herbert & Cooper, Ltd offered their Premier Military Safety as the 1890 ultimate in lightweight, fast, and reliable military cycling. (*Dr. William E. Bagwell*)

In the 1890s the Army turned out this rare military tandem, which needed double manpower. It was equipped with a repeating rifle, Colt revolvers, a set of signal flags, overcoats, and blankets. (*Dr. William E. Bagwell*)

On July 3, 1897, Lieutenant Moss held a final review of his troops before embarking on the historic journey of 1,900 miles from Fort Missoula, Montana, to St. Louis, Missouri. (*Army & Navy Journal*)

25th Infantry Bicycle Corps as the long overland trip to St. Louis began. (*Army & Navy Journal*)

An Italian army bicycle squad departing Trevin, Italy, for the front lines in World War I. (*U.S. Signal Corps*)

Canadian soldiers riding to the front—on their way to a captured French town in World War I. (*U.S. Signal Corps*)

Italian scouting team well up in the front lines on bicycle patrol. Thirty-caliber, water-cooled machine gun is set up on one bike as mobile mount. (*U.S. Signal Corps*)

French army field kitchen in frontline area in World War I. Such units used bicycles heavily for transportation and for carrying supplies. (*U.S. Signal Corps*)

Bicycle repairs being made under desperate conditions: German cycle orderlies trying to get their machines ready to roll as shells explode all about them in the shattered village of Etreillers, on April 25, 1917. (*Imperial War Museum, London*)

A fully equipped bicycle scout team moving out for reconnaissance on the Toutencourt Contay Road on April 13, 1918. (*Imperial War Museum, London*)

Moving after the Germans: British cyclists and cavalry passing through the ruined village of Brie in March 1917. (*Imperial War Museum, London*)

March 1917 in the village of Vraignes. British cyclist troops helping to move children away from the line of fire. (*Imperial War Museum, London*)

4

The Biscuit-and-Bean March

Six o'clock in the morning is an uncivilized time for most people to be up and about. But in the Montana countryside surrounding Fort Missoula, six A.M., in 1897 was well past the time when ranchers and farmers were already hard at work. These good people were accustomed to considerable activity at this time of day, and wagons and farming equipment had long since taken to the roads.

On the morning of Monday, June 14, 1897, just about everyone who looked at the main road leading away from Missoula came to a dead halt in his work. Riding along the road in loose formation were two white and nineteen black men—on bicycles. Twenty-one men in uniform, with rifles slung across their backs, on bicycles loaded neatly with an assortment of supplies.

It was the beginning of a historic 1,900-mile trek by bicycle, under conditions deliberately chosen to test the mettle of the men and their two-wheel machines. Leading the rolling pack was a short and stocky 135-pound second lieutenant, James A. Moss, the man whom historians were to say was to the bicycle what Lindbergh was to aviation.

Jim Moss had a profound streak of practicality in him. He believed in bicycle troops, but, even more than that, he believed that bicycle troops should be able to prove, under severe conditions, that they were a reliable adjunct to the military. His favorite words seem to be practical, reliable, durable. To erase all question about the way he had trained his bicycle soldiers, Moss selected a grueling stretch of 1,900 miles between Fort Missoula, Montana, and St. Louis, Missouri, over which his men were to carry out a forced march on their bikes.

The route took in low and high altitudes, both dry and wet climates, and with a variety of road surfaces that ranged from flat to hilly and, on occasion, to steep grades. There were the stony and mountainous roads of Montana, the hummocky dirt roads of Wyoming and South Dakota, the sandy roads of Nebraska, and the clay wagon ruts of Missouri.

Moss led his men from the fort at 5:30 A.M. on June 14, 1897, convinced that he'd take them all the way to St. Louis. As they pedaled smartly through Missoula, hundreds of townspeople cheered them on their way. Once before they'd seen Moss off on a long cycle journey. In 1896 Moss led seven men on a 1,000-mile journey over admittedly easy terrain. But it was an excellent trip from the fort down through Yellowstone National Park, and a return via Fort Assiniboine. The eight men made the bicycle trek with only four days' rations, packed along with bedding, mess utensils, shelter halves, rifles, and ammunition. Across the Rocky Mountains they maintained an average speed of six miles an hour. They rode through rain and mud, and to the cyclist force the sight of roaring geysers in Yellowstone was a shower of success.

But this was the test. The 25th Infantry Bicycle Corps

was about to tackle 1,900 miles, with its men in excellent condition and banking their reputation on the all-new Spalding bikes, built to specifications laid down by Moss. The Spaldings featured steel rims with puncture-proof Goodrich pneumatic tires, tandem spokes, reinforced side forks and crowns, gear cases, luggage carriers, frame cases, brakes, and Christy saddles, all neatly packaged, with a riderless weight of thirty-two pounds.

Normally Moss would have been the only white man with his bicycle troop. But there was another. Assistant Surgeon J. M. Kennedy. Regulations called for at least one medical officer to be part of the twenty-one-man command. Kennedy, who was less than enthusiastic about the trip, was selected. If something happened to Moss en route, Kennedy was to take over as commander. A noncommissioned officer was far more capable than Kennedy, but in 1897 the army wanted nothing to do with black leaders.

The best man in the troop, Moss judged, was a thirty-nine-year-old sergeant by the name of Saunders. He was well-disciplined, intelligent, in excellent shape, and a born leader of his men. Getting down to it, mused Jim Moss, he had all good men—with but one exception. Pvt. Eugene Jones was a chronic whiner, almost a nonstop complainer. Moss shrugged off the problem; he'd handled that sort before.

Moss had in his command Sergeant Saunders, Corporal Martin, and Privates F. Johnson, S. Johnson, Proctor, Cook, Haines, Findley, Bridges, Scott, Dingman, S. Williamson, W. Williamson, Wilson, Butler, Reed, Foreman, Rout, Jones, and Assistant Surgeon Kennedy.

Each fully equipped bike, with supplies, averaged fifty-nine pounds. Moss worked out every detail for the reports he was to file. The heaviest soldier, stripped, weighed 177 pounds, the lightest just over 125 pounds, for an average of 148.5 pounds per man. This put more than 200 pounds per bicycle on the road, but the men were in good condition and well-trained. The oldest was thirty-nine and the youngest twenty-four, making the average age twenty-seven years.

Strangely enough, Moss was in violation of army regulations because of his bigger men. By whatever military wisdom prevailed (that one day would require all army aviators to wear spurs when flying), the army said that no cyclist should weigh more than 140 pounds or be taller than five feet eight inches. Moss appealed to Maj. Gen. Nelson A. Miles to waive the regulations for the trip and the general, sharing Moss's enthusiasm for the venture, agreed.

Evidence of Moss's meticulous preparations was to be found in the equipment his men carried. Cooking pans were shaped to fit diamond-shaped carrying pouches, and each man carried his own tin cup, plate, knife, fork, and spoon. Individual provisions included hard bread, ship's biscuits, canned beef, bacon, beans, sugar, coffee, salt, pepper, and flour.

Each man also carried a Krag-Jorgenson rifle (except one individualist who received permission to tote his own shotgun), with fifty rounds of ammunition in his cartridge belt. Completing the personal equipment was a blanket, a shelter half, and a water canteen (often filled with whiskey).

Along the bicycle route, Moss arranged for a resupply station every 100 miles. Most supplies were shipped ahead by rail. Finally, every last detail had been met. It was time to move out.

The first stretch went beautifully. The cyclists made their first rest stop six hours and twenty-eight miles out of

Fort Missoula. Moss dispersed his men beneath heavy shade trees alongside a ranch and broke for lunch. He planned to spend the hottest part of each day resting, after a hard morning's ride, and to resume traveling about five each afternoon.

The planning was great, but not the weather. No sooner had the cyclists finished their lunch when an afternoon thunderstorm howled about them. Before the men could set up their small tents they were inundated. Lightning cast its eerie shafts of light all about them and the men decided to wait out the storm beneath the huge branches of the trees they had selected for shade.

With the passing of the storm the drenched cyclists started out to make up for loss time. Wet or not, Moss wanted no undue delay this early in the march. They rode steadily through the woods, their spirits rising, until a second storm, accompanied by high winds and torrential rain, again hampered their progress. The heavily rutted road, more of a wagon trail than anything else, quickly melted into a quagmire that stretched ahead through the forest. Continued movement became so difficult that Moss, ever the opportunist, ordered his troops off the road to avoid the mud, and set them to pushing their bicycles through weeds and underbrush that offered less resistance.

It took two hours of strenuous pushing and scrambling to get through the storm-drenched area. By the time the weather had cleared, the men were exhausted and Moss called a halt. After a brief rest they remounted their bikes and pedaled along still-muddy and hilly trails, passing the Clear Water Post Office at dusk. Relentlessly, Moss pressed on. Not until eight that night did he terminate the first day's trek, pitching camp at Cottonwood, just over fifty-four miles from Fort Missoula.

If anything, the second day was worse than its predecessor, for even though the heavy rains had relaxed to a drizzle, the narrow road had become an impassable river of mud. There was just no way to continue. Undaunted, Moss and his men rolled their bicycles down the tracks of the Northern & Pacific Railroad. They dragged themselves along in this fashion for nine miles, until they reached Elliston, Montana. Splattered with mud, drenched to the skin, weary, they pitched their tent halves to wait out the storm.

Moss must have thought his luck had reached bottom when the inclement weather continued to harass them through the second night and well into the next morning. With rations running low, he pushed his men to head for Fort Harrison, where they were to resupply—and perhaps get a decent weather break. It was back to the railroad tracks and a jolting, muscle-pounding trek. Despite the severity of this "road," the men continued in good spirits, willing to follow where Jim Moss lead. All except Pvt. Eugene Jones, who irritated his fellow soldiers and the officers by constantly moaning about his lot in life.

Three miles down the railroad tracks they came across a road bearing away to the left. Moss called a halt while he studied the old Mullan Stage Road. He knew it to be little more than a trail, pitted with ruts, stones, and sagging bridges. Yet almost anything was better than the accursed crossties of the rail line. Moss took the road, leading his men by pushing his own bicycle up the first slope of slippery mud.

It was worse than Moss could have imagined. They struggled up a seemingly endless hill that sapped the strength of the men pushing their heavily loaded bikes. Two hours and seven miles later they reached the summit of the Main Divide of the Rocky Mountains. The men looked about them with disbelief. The hour was high noon and it was the last week of spring. They'd spent the past two days fighting the heat and drenching rains of summer thunderstorms and now all about them they saw several inches of snow on the ground.

There was hardly time for a few muttered curses when a freezing sleet slashed down at them from the leaden sky. Moss rushed them from the summit to get to warmer air, but the temperature dropped so swiftly that every five or ten minutes the men had to stop to rub freezing hands and ears.

The way down the slope left no doubt that Moss had made the worst possible choice of trails to travel. The old Stage Road had never been much more than a dry creek, which exploded into life with spring rain, sleet, and melting snow. Now the men worked their way slowly and carefully down a road filled with water and slush above their ankles, exerting a constant grip on their heavy bicycles to prevent them from getting away.

Four-and-a-half hours after starting down the mountain slope Moss and his men dragged themselves into Fort Harrison. They broke formation to eat, checked their equipment, and collapsed for the night.

The men awoke to unexpectedly clear skies. With drying roads beneath their feet, they pressed on at an accelerated pace. By the time their trek ended at nightfall they had covered more than their planned fifty miles, and set up camp in a construction area called Recap, located between the Northern & Pacific Railroad tracks and the Gallatin River.

Morning light brought groans from the men. On one side of their planned travel route rose a high bluff. The river

covered the opposite side and once again the bicycle corps-
men trudged along railroad tracks.

They rode and pushed their way for five jolting miles
over new crossties, the spaces between the newly installed
logs still unfilled and tamped down with earth. If only they
could move alongside the tracks, but there was no way—
the railbed was a mess of old crossties, and heaped dirt
and rocks on both sides. They could feel their muscles
tightening as they fought their way ahead, finally covering
the five miles to Gallatin, Montana, by midmorning.

Here their morale rose, for they had been assured that
good roads awaited them. But beyond Gallatin the "good
road" turned out to be a blind trail through marshy fields
buzzing with vicious mosquitos.

Off they went, into the worst segment of the trip so far,
maddened by the incessant bites of swarming insects. No
matter how fast they pedaled the mosquitos stayed with
them, causing intense suffering from swollen eyes, faces,
necks, and hands.

Just west of Logan, they swerved away from the marshy
trail to follow the rail tracks into town, and another two
hours of pedaling brought them to Bozeman, center of the
Gallatin Valley.

Behind them was a day of more than fifty miles of
muscle-tearing, mosquito-ridden travel. And they had ticked
off only a small part of the journey to come.

On June 23, nine days out of their home base, the 25th
Infantry Bicycle Corps rode into Billings, Montana. It was
a little before 10 A.M. In four hours of hard riding that
morning the men had sped over thirty-seven miles. They
pedaled into Billings in high spirits.

At the local rail depot they picked up the supplies waiting for them. Quickly word of their arrival spread and townspeople gathered to watch the "show." Seeing nineteen black men in uniform on bicycles brought forth catcalls and derisive laughter, and an angry Moss led his men quickly out of the town.

Moss must have felt that someone was jinxing them. Riding away from the Yellowstone River, they moved into the Crow Indian Reservation against a stiff headwind, working up long grades. Before Moss and his men knew what was happening, they were surrounded by whooping Crows, having the time of their lives making fun of this soldier infantry on bicycles. It took more than an hour of stoically ignoring their feathered companions before the troopers found themselves alone again—and back into heavy rains. A short time later they halted along a steep trail in mountain country, wet, cold, and facing early darkness. Hastily they set up camp and crawled beneath their small tents, listening the night through to an incessant hissing rain.

Moss realized that to slow down now could cripple the expedition. The men had to keep moving. As they ate a quick breakfast, the rains eased and finally stopped. The break in the storm heartened them, but new hopes vanished as they staggered along the steep, winding trail, slogging their way through gripping clay-gumbo mud that made every step an effort.

The entire day ground slowly forward. Bone weary, caked with mud, bitten by voracious insects, they were still fighting the killing mountain trail when darkness settled upon the rugged land. They made camp and collapsed into deep sleep.

They were awake at dawn and started another grueling

session along the winding and hilly trail, stopping frequently to scrape caked mud from bicycle wheels and frames.

They were still on the trail when night fell. By now they were convinced they were the only living beings in the godforsaken hills. They were so fed up with the trail they decided to push on as long as they could in darkness. Two-and-a-half hours later they stumbled onto the banks of Pryor Creek. No disillusionment with the task of fording the stream. It was a joy compared to the mountain trail—and the water washed the heavy mud from their bikes. Across the stream they came upon a deserted Indian cabin where the men fell asleep in their clothes.

By now their supplies were almost gone. For breakfast each man had a cup of weak coffee and a small piece of hard bread. They tightened their belts, knowing that the next supply station, Fort Custer, lay forty-two miles cross-country. Their spirits sagged further when their first three hours of fighting through still more mud gained them only six miles.

Then they crested a ridge and saw Moss's weary features break out in a huge grin. The lieutenant pointed ahead. Before them lay a hard, dry surface—and a downhill slope. Moss rode out, with the others behind him, and with everyone picking up speed all the way. At three-thirty that afternoon they pedaled into Fort Custer. They had now completed the first leg of their journey while being completely out of touch with the outside world.

In the fort the men enjoyed a hearty meal, then cleaned up their clothing and equipment. Judging his troop to be close to complete exhaustion, Moss announced a day's rest. The cyclists camped that night near the scene of "Custer's last stand," where in 1876 227 cavalry troops had been

wiped out in a bloody fight with Sioux and Cheyenne Indians. They spent their day of rest sightseeing along the
Little Big Horn.

Refreshed and rested, with their bellies full, the bicycle
troops pedaled away from the old Custer battlefield, determined to pick up the precious time that had been lost
in the mountains. They were now moving from Montana
into Wyoming, and at the crossing from one state to another was an imaginary signpost marking the first third of
their journey of 1,900 miles. It was a good thing they'd had
their rest—the ninety miles from the Little Big Horn to
Sheridan, Wyoming, proved to be one of the most difficult
legs of their trek.

What was laughingly called a road snaked through rough
and hilly country, trying its best—and failing—to follow
the river to the Wyoming border. Six times Moss and his
cyclists came to a stop, staring morosely at the water before them, and each time they had to ford the Little Big
Horn, wading chest-high through water in teams of four—
carrying their bicycles across one by one, raised high
above their heads on long poles.

Grimly determined now to successfully combat whatever
nature had to offer, the twenty-one men hammered their
way to the Wyoming border. Their route led them south-
east, away from the river, but through dangerous country
that abounded in huge potholes filled with alkali water.
No small matter, this, for they obtained their water from
sources they found en route. Their main supplies came
from railroad tanks they passed.

Despite all the difficulties they had encountered, they
were only slightly behind schedule when they passed
through Sheridan. They pressed forward and on June 29,

after having battled their way up twenty miles of mountain grade, tortured by a broiling sun, the 25th Infantry Bicycle Corps pedaled wearily into Gillette, Wyoming.

Moss grinned at his men. "Time for lunch," he announced.

As his men rested, Moss checked the route ahead. Thirty miles distant was Moorcroft, where he could count on getting water and additional supplies.

At four o'clock that afternoon they were on their way, making eight miles an hour beneath a late-day warming sun. Just after six P.M. things started coming unglued. Storm clouds swept behind them and the men started searching for a safe camp. At that moment they all heard a sharp metallic *snap!* Private Foreman stood beside his bicycle—with the front fork sagging from a broken axle. Moss tried not to show his frustration. They had no spare front axles. Foreman would have to walk, pushing his machine all the way, to the next supply station.

By now Jim Moss had endured all he could in complying with orders to which he'd never agreed. He turned the command over to Sergeant Saunders.

"Keep the men together," ordered Moss. "Proceed to Moorcroft with the speed it takes Foreman to walk his machine. I'm going ahead with the cook and two men. We'll get a hot meal together and line up repair materials and supplies."

Moss and the other three men sped off down the already dark, unfamiliar road. They made only four miles before the black night and muddy surface forced them to dismount. Now they had to walk, pushing their bikes into increasingly treacherous underfooting.

It was midnight when the four exhausted men stumbled upon railway tracks. Hungry and cold from the damp night air, they sprawled on the ground to rest. They needed warmth but failed to find firewood. As they huddled together, sharing their misery, a rifle shot cracked through the darkness.

"Fire one shot," Moss ordered a soldier. Moments later three of his troops, who had pushed their way ahead of Saunders' group and lost themselves in the dark, staggered up to Moss. Now they made up a band of seven, with fourteen more coming up behind. Moss and the six soldiers started out in the darkness for Moorcroft.

The pain of pulled muscles was excruciating. Every man suffered from muscle cramps. Doggedly and deliberately they pushed on. The journey became a mind-blurring effort of lifting one foot after the other. Then, after hours of body-punishing travel, a voice groaned from the darkness.

"My God . . . I cain't . . . I cain't go no more."

Moss turned but couldn't see a thing in the inky night. Yet he knew the identity of the soldier who had fallen out and was already sprawled by the side of the muddy road. "Leave him there," he ordered. "Let him sleep."

Moss resumed the march. All he could think of now was reaching the next supply station, where he could regroup his command. His men were strung out along fifteen miles of muddy Wyoming trail. He stumbled on, more asleep than awake, his bicycle as much a support to his shaking body as it was a burden to push. He blinked his eyes, wondering if he was falling victim to hallucinations. In the distance there semed to be a faint glow of light, as if a clothesline were strung before the road, drifting toward him. It came so close it seemed certain to strike his face. Several times he threw out his arm, but nothing was there.

Jim Moss fell asleep even as he fought his way through the mud. His feet stumbled and he went down, as if in slow motion, unconscious but still trying to walk. The six men with him went down like poled oxen. Each soldier slept where he fell.

Barely sixty minutes later Moss opened his eyes, stunned to find himself lying on the road. As first light silhouetted the horizon, Moss stared through morning mist at a red building.

Moorcroft! *And only a few steps away from where they'd fallen into the mud.*

Angered and disgusted with himself, Moss shouted at the other men to get to their feet. With stiffened arms and legs they lurched into the supply camp. The cook ordered the men with him to help. Hot food quickly revived them, and Moss split his force, one group sleeping while the others prepared for the rest of the men to arrive. One by one the rear guard straggled in, grateful for the hot meal waiting for them.

By two o'clock that same afternoon, the 25th Infantry Bicycle Corps was again on its way. Jim Moss knew many things. But not how to quit.

For the next five days the bicycle troop traveled steadily across the southwestern corner of South Dakota. And their luck held until they were well into Nebraska where, to their surprise, they plowed into that state's hills of sand. Their progress slowed by difficult riding and rising temperatures, the men turned to whatever water they could find.

Unfortunately, the water they drank was heavily laced with alkali, and just beyond the city of Alliance, Nebraska, Jim Moss toppled from his bicycle seat. Half unconscious and seriously ill from taking too much alkali into his system, he was judged unfit for further travel by bicycle. Assistant Surgeon J. M. Kennedy now took over command of the troop. The men carried Moss back to Alliance where he could recover and, later, could travel by train to rejoin his command.

Kennedy must have regretted the twist of fate that gave him control of the soldier cyclists, for no sooner was Moss removed from his position of leadership than the troop plunged into a fresh nightmare. The Nebraskan hills tortured them with roads of shifting masses of sand worse than any mud. Every day the sun blazed hotter in the sky, sapping their strength and burning whatever skin was exposed to its brutal rays. Finally human endurance reached its limit, and Kennedy led the men away from the ankle-deep sand to follow the railroad tracks.

Ahead of the men lay 170 miles of torturous travel. It was a question of which was worse, the jarring of the railroad crossties or the ankle-clutching sand.

On July 7, as the men fell by the tracks to rest beneath trees, the temperature registered 110° F. in the shade. That night more than half the men were seriously ill. Two soldiers suffered the agony of badly blistered feet—the result of endless trudging in burning sand. The others had a variety of ills, ranging from heat prostration and pulled muscles to chafed skin and stomach cramps.

Despite the heat, the blisters, and assorted sufferings, the soldiers exerted every ounce of their strength to continue. What carried them through the worst of the trek was the clean water they drew from the railroad storage tanks. They pushed their way through the worst of the sand hills in four-and-a-half days, establishing the astonishing average of better than thirty-seven miles a day.

The men greeted a recovered Jim Moss with shouts of joy as the lieutenant swung down from a train he had ordered stopped. With Moss again in command, they reached the clay roads of Missouri on July 17. They rolled into the town of Rulo, where they discovered that the local citizens were every bit as hostile as the country through which they'd just fought their way. The local folk, it seemed, wanted no truck with "nigras," even if they were soldiers.

The sand hills were behind them, and so were the mountains, but nothing had improved where the roads were concerned. They crossed the state on what Moss later described as the worst roads of the entire journey.

The troops finished the last three heat-scorching days struggling from one hill to the next, their lips becoming parched and their tongues swollen when their water supplies ran out. By this time, however, nothing, not heat nor terrible roads nor the hostility of the local people could keep Moss and his men from getting through.

No matter that almost all of Missouri regarded them as outcasts. St. Louis made it up to them with a thundering reception and open arms. Waiting to greet them was a huge crowd of cheering well-wishers on bicycles, who provided a colorful escort for the men.

They officially ended their memorable trip of 1,900 miles before the Cottage Hotel in Forest Park. It was six o'clock on the evening of Saturday, July 24, 1897. Exclusive of the brief time spent in repairs and recuperating from illness, they had completed their journey in thirty-four days of actual travel, averaging 6.3 miles an hour and 55.9 miles a day.

Jim Moss was the hero of the day. He told reporters he was convinced that the trip had demonstrated the ability of an army bicycle corps to compete with infantry or cavalry moving cross-country at one-third of the cost.

"Some of our experiences," he stressed, "tested to the utmost not only the men's physical endurance, but also their moral courage and disposition. I wish to commend them for the spirit, pluck, and fine soldierly qualities they displayed."

Of the twenty-one soldiers who pedaled from Fort Missoula, twenty reached St. Louis in surprisingly good health and condition. Only one man failed to complete the trip. One week short of their destination, Pvt. Eugene Jones claimed to be too weak to continue. Moss shipped Jones and his bicycle back to Fort Missoula by train.

No one missed him. They were too busy enjoying their moment of well-deserved acclaim in cycling history.

5

The Bicycle Goes to War

The bicycle managed to survive three decades of trial-and-error military experiments before actually being committed to battle. But going to war on two-wheelers was actually a two-phase affair, the first being a too-late entry into Cuba, and the second being a full-scale test in South Africa.

The initial orders for combat service came with the Spanish-American War of 1898, and once again it brought into the limelight none other than Lt. James Moss and his men of the 25th Infantry Bicycle Corps.

When Moss completed his epic journey from Montana to Missouri, his hopes for realistic tests for bicycle troops fell by the wayside. He soon found himself a cyclist leader with no one to lead, and an officer without a command.

On his return to Fort Missoula, Moss prepared an official proposal for an unprecedented and, he considered, a really acid test of the bicycle under field conditions. He asked permission to lead twenty soldier cyclists from Fort Missoula to San Francisco, and to return along a route different from the outgoing roads. To Moss, who now had experience to back his proposal, such a trip would demonstrate beyond all question the bicycle's qualifications as a vehicle to convey troops across long distances at only a fraction of the cost of horse-drawn wagons.

Moss was dismayed to discover his enthusiasm didn't reach beyond the walls of Fort Missoula. The Secretary of War, who passed upon such matters, had little interest in soldiers pedaling their way around the country. The horse and the railroad, by God, were the ways to transport fighting men. Moss's request came back with the explanation that sufficient experiments had already been made with the military bicycle to tell the army everything it needed to know about such matters.

Sorely disappointed, Moss swallowed his pride and returned to the mundane life of an army post officer, while the black cyclists who had made history with him returned to their prosaic duties.

Yet "prosaic" was a matter of attitude. The black soldiers' regiment was at the time the only organized force in the northwestern United States, and much of their time was spent away from their post, helping people recover from the ravages of weather and man. They assisted people caught in floods, fires, and storms. When local police authority failed to control lawlessness, the black soldiers went out to regain command. They assisted Indian agents in a wide range of duties. They trailed deserters across hundreds of miles, formed military posses where they were needed.

At times such duty was the best a soldier could have, for the men often set up camps deep in California's Yosemite, Sequoia, and Grant national parks. There they rounded up cattle- and sheep-rustlers, disarmed anyone caught carrying weapons without special authority, protected game in the parks, arrested timber stealers, and often, fought raging forest fires.

Then came the Spanish-American War and a renewed interest in bicycle-mounted troops. Moss received orders to regroup his force. Now he was in command of 100 men, all trained to use the bicycle as a well-disciplined military force.

Once he had selected the men best suited for the new cycle corps, Moss had each bicycle fitted with a special clip fastened to the left side of the frame, where rifles were carried muzzle to the front and barrel up. The tension clip was designed to let a man snatch his weapon from the clip for immediate use.

Moss had learned his lessons well on his 1,900-mile trip, when the weight and clumsiness of a rifle slung across a man's back was nearly too much to endure along with other privations. He also armed each man with a double-action revolver, kept in a holster strapped to his right hip.

Moss never went to war with the 25th Infantry Bicycle Corps. The war didn't last long enough. Lt. Col. Theodore Roosevelt and his cavalry troop of Rough Riders stormed San Juan Hill and three months after the war began it was ended. The Army took up occupation duties in Cuba.

Resigned to remaining forever in Montana, Moss was surprised when he received emergency orders for shipping out to Cuba. All hell had broken loose in Havana. In the wet summer season there was an explosive spread of yellow fever and a mild form of malaria. Cubans and occupying American troops alike were affected, but the local citizens heaped blame on the United States Army, taking to the streets with mob violence and riots. The United States hastily withdrew its own stricken soldiers and Maj. Gen. Nelson A. Miles sent out a call for Moss and his all-new bicycle force.

Two days later Moss and his 100 picked men were on a train to Tampa, Florida, where they moved quickly aboard a waiting troopship. No sooner had they disembarked in

Havana than they were rushed into immediate riot-control duty.

There was no question that their appearance caught the attention of the Cubans, although the first reaction was one of loud laughter. The sight of black soldiers on bicycles wheeling to scenes of trouble brought its mixture of scorn and amusement. The chuckles died away when they watched the disciplined order of Moss and his men who, heavily armed, rode unflinchingly into the worst trouble spots in the Cuban city. For a while the Cubans held back. Then the incidence of fever increased sharply and amused tolerance exploded again into anger.

Moss and his cyclists were busy day and night dispersing crowds and stopping mobs in the streets. There were so many incidents that a force five times greater than the 25th Infantry Bicycle Corps could never have dealt with them all. Yet wherever Moss and his men appeared they put down the rioting mobs. Their technique was to approach in groups from different sides of the crowd, who suddenly found themselves facing a hundred heavily armed and determined men. If the cyclists encountered a crowd that seemed determined to break through their ranks, the men would dismount, stack their bicycles into a barricade, and present a solid force of firepower.

Against all the pessimistic forecasts for a force of only a hundred men, the Moss troop was given credit as the major factor in stopping a potential destruction in its tracks. Oddly enough, the bicycle troops never had to resort to their weapons. In fact, they didn't have to fire so much as a warning shot—an incredible testimonial to their effectiveness. The men stayed on twenty-four-hour duty until the outbreak of fever subsided and the threat of mob outbreaks eased away.

Moss and his men returned to Montana with their weapons unused, but with a ringing tribute to the effectiveness of military bicycle forces.

Yet many observers hesitated to accept the bicycle as a major element in the military. Riot duty was one thing, they noted, not without justification. Combat was another. That test was to come just one year later.

War broke out in 1899 on the plains of South Africa. It was called the Boer War after the Dutch farmers of that land who decided to implement armed resistance against the British advance into the territories of the area. Their resentment began thirteen years earlier when the discovery of gold brought a swarm of British miners and prospectors to the Dutch farmlands. To control the newcomers the Boer government refused them citizenship and imposed severe taxes on almost every activity in which they engaged.

The British, as might have been expected, vigorously protested such shabby treatment, accepting the moves of the Boers as a direct challenge to the Crown. The situation went from bad to worse when, in 1895, Sir Leander Starr Jameson carried out an unexpected military raid against the Boers. The Dutch on their part shouted that the Jameson raid was an ill-concealed British attempt to seize the Transvaal. In mutual self-interest the locals immediately formed a military alliance of the Transvaal and the Orange Free State.

One action begets another. The British reacted with the claim that the alliance was a subterfuge to deny deserved commercial rights to their citizens, and demanded the disbanding of the new alliance and the withdrawal of military forces. No one yielded and on October 12, 1899, both sides plunged into open conflict.

Perhaps the single most important piece of equipment brought to South Africa by the British military force was the bicycle. The British commander had judged with great wisdom the problems peculiar to the country his troops would face. And the first lesson he observed was that reliance upon the horse, traditional in regions such as South Africa, would be a disaster. The mortality rate among such animals was nothing less than crippling. To have based his field operations upon horse-mounted troops, with the loss of the horses through disease and sickness, could have crippled his men and left them at the mercy of their enemies.

At the same time, he needed mobility. The nature of the land called for great flexibility in moving his forces from one danger point to another. For this purpose the British made their gamble on the bicycle. If they were right, then British troops would be able to move with much greater speed than could the Boer soldiers, and the British would enjoy the advantage of being able to select their battlegrounds, as well as being able to press after enemy forces.

Thousands of bicycles arrived with the British. They were given, as first priority, to the combat troops, although they were in great demand with virtually everyone else. The bicycle carried supplies, permitted rapid communication and transport, and served as a substitute for horses, without the attendant problems of food supplies and diseased animals.

The bicycle became synonymous with the British in South Africa and prompted one African, upon seeing his first bicycle under way with a British soldier riding serenely by, to comment: "Trust the English to invent a way of traveling while sitting down."

During its initial use in South Africa, the bicycle faced many of the problems other military forces had encountered in the field. The machines were heavy, required excessive maintenance and, unless surface conditions were reasonable, they often had to be abandoned by troops who were forced to keep moving in field operations.

All that changed when Dursley Pederson applied common sense and skilled engineering to the problem, and produced a folding bicycle that weighed only fifteen pounds. Soldiers who were issued the new machines quickly devised carrying straps and slings for the folded bicycles, and overnight the problems of moving through terrain impassable to any wheeled vehicle disappeared. On good terrain the troops could travel from forty to sixty miles a day with full equipment. When they encountered uncharted and rough surfaces, the men folded their bicycles into a compact and manageable size, lashed them to their backs, and kept moving on foot.

The moment they were back on reasonable ground, the folded machines were reassembled, and the men were moving swiftly in pursuit of their enemy. No force on foot could hope to escape the cyclist troops. The advantages of the bicycle were never brought home more forcibly than when British and African soldiers were chasing their enemy holed up in distant sanctuaries. So long as the Boers knew the general distance of their camps from the British and Africans, they assumed they had a built-in time safety factor. But too often they judged that time on the basis of troops on foot.

They were completely unprepared for the silent swift strikes of men on bicycles. The British and African cycle troops covered ground quickly, and were able to move into encirclement positions without detection by their unsuspecting foes. Then they had the choice of swift attack, often firing from moving bicycles for surprise effect, or moving up close to their enemy and making a rush on foot.

A year later the war was considered all but ended. The British landed heavy reinforcements under the command of Lord Kitchener, and the newly arrived troops moved across South Africa in a well-planned mopping-up maneuver. The campaign fizzled out when the Boers chose not to stand and fight. Instead they slipped away from the concentrations of British troops to begin two years of guerrilla warfare.

Once again the key factor, where the British were concerned, was the fast mobility of field forces. And the bicycle became the critical element of that mobility. Kitchener's troops were forced to comb the guerrilla country section by section. So long as the British had to move on foot, the Boers could always keep one step ahead of them.

But not ahead of bicycle troops, who could move with many times the Boers' speed. If they remained holed up, the British had plenty of time to move in heavy siege forces. If the Boers fled, they were sure to be overtaken by hundreds of fresh, heavily armed men on bicycles.

Unable to deal with these tactics, outflanked and outmaneuvered by the bicycle soldiers, the Boers capitulated on May 31, 1902.

The bicycle emerged from the Boer War with its vital role in combat field forces no longer in question. Theory had been replaced with performance. Questions had been shunted aside by victories. The bicycle had ridden off to war an unknown machine, but it emerged from its first major conflict with flying colors. It proved able to travel where no horse had ever penetrated. It conquered South Africa's densest brush, rolled along its narrow trails, and sped across fields and roads quickly and silently, demanding no more support than a lubricating can and a pocket wrench.

The military bicycle had come of age.

Japanese army combat troops line up their bicycle brigade for inspection before moving out on maneuvers (about 1938). (*U.S. Infantry Journal*)

German cyclist forces on maneuvers in the late 1930s demonstrate that it takes only seconds for a cyclist to become an infantryman, as they storm a high bluff. (*U.S. Infantry Journal*)

Soviet troops intended for fast scouting operations, before leaving for maneuvers in the 1930s. The cyclist troops are shown with their war dogs in review in Moscow's Red Square. (*U.S. Infantry Journal*)

British cyclist troops, in training just before World War II, line up for an "organizational portrait." (*Imperial War Museum, London*)

British bicycle troops on cross-country maneuvers just before World
War II. (*Imperial War Museum, London*)

Bicycles by the hundreds were dumped on streets and highways by
retreating soldiers as the Belgian army fell apart under heavy German
pressure early in World War II. (*Wide World Photos*)

German infantrymen stay under cover after being pinned down by Norwegian mountain troops firing from ambush, as German tanks roll up to break the deadlock. (*Wide World Photos*)

Combat troops of the "Bicycle Division" in January 1942 roll southward in the Philippines on their way to Manila. (*U.S. Army*)

Fitted out in an impermeable protective suit, a German chemical warfare soldier inspects his bicycle-mounted poison gas detection kit. (*U.S. Infantry Journal*)

This German soldier, captured on December 23, 1944, by troops of the 3rd Armored Division, had used his bicycle for hit-and-run attacks that killed twenty-two American soldiers. (*U.S. Army*)

As American forces hurled back dug-in Japanese troops in the Philippines, Filipino guerrillas rode in from the hills to coordinate the fighting with the U.S. troops, April 4, 1945. (*U.S. Army*)

German soldiers riding their bicycles to a prisoner-of-war collection point along the Brenner Pass in Bolzano Province, Italy, in 1945. (*U.S. Army*)

Thousands of bicycles dropped off by surrendering German troops near Loire, France. Picture taken on September 17, 1944. *U.S. Army*

Troops of the 84th Infantry (Railsplitter) Division using captured German bicycles along the front, near Rickelrath, Germany, on February 28, 1945. (*U.S. Army*)

6

Along the Trenches

The first light of day came reluctantly, as if it preferred the hiding cloak of darkness. Yet the earth rolled ponderously about its axis, and no wish or hope could stay the thin sliver of gray that began to splinter the eastern horizon. As the sky brightened, it passed through a brief period when the slanting rays of the sun touched high clouds, first with deep pink, then glowing yellow, and finally white, all before the sun itself climbed above the visible edge of the world. In that quiet moment hundreds of thousands of men lifted their eyes upward, regretting the brightness that would follow, that would reveal to them the scarred horror of a world gone mad. For in the area of France where the river Marne flowed, terrible things had been done to the earth, now lying stark in the growing.day.

The fields and the farms, the banks of streams and the slopes of gentle hills, the orchards and valleys, all had been attacked and laid bare to their earthly bones. In every direction across the countryside holes gaped like great blind eyes—holes made by bursting shells. Slicing crazily through the mindless pattern of destruction were other scars, zigzag things carved from the soil by men desperate to escape the reach of jacketed steel and glowing fragments and powder that shattered all about it, especially the fragile bodies of men.

Yet, despite the disease that scarred the land, there was still beauty to be found. It was fleeting, to be sure, and not all men who looked upon it saw the same thing. To some it was beauty. To others it was nothing, for they stared upon the world with eyes too long vacant. And finally, to another group of hard-eyed men, the beauty that was the early morning mist gliding from the Marne River was a gossamer shield behind which they might conceal themselves from enemies.

On the south side of the Marne was a group of men with bicycles. Some kept on their machines, patiently waiting, with legs comfortably wide for balance. Others had left their cycles and sat or sprawled on the ground, awaiting the signal that would galvanize them into action. But all of them studied the mist that drifted from the rippling gray surface of the Marne. The cottony soft mist sheathed river and surrounding countryside in a hush of its own making. At a touch of breeze the mist swirled, sending tendrils exploring upward along the river banks, reaching high enough to glide along the lower structure of a bridge spanning the river and into the village of Mt. St. Pere.

There was a false security in that mist. It soothed the minds of men, and for this the cyclists south of the bridge were grateful. They were Germans, and they were deep in the land of their French enemy. The mist also lulled the French into a pervasive security that was perilously thin and insubstantial.

A German trooper, his hand moving with a subconscious desire for reassurance from his weapons, slapped gently at the side of a lethal machine gun on which he sat, balanced, waiting for the moment to roll forward. The trooper nodded to himself. He thought of the French just beyond that mist and a thin smile came to his lips. Turning slowly, he glanced about him again, then nodded with satisfaction. His men, soldiers of the 1st Bicycle Company, Rifleman Battalion of the Guards of the German army, had traveled a long way through a treacherous night.

In the midst of the enemy, the German cyclists had struggled through more than twenty miles of muddy roads, unexpected embankments, and open fields. They had managed to escape the attention of French patrols and to work their way through mine fields. Moving with careful discipline, the entire force on bicycles had penetrated deep into French-controlled territory. Now, looking down from a slope on the iron-and-concrete bridge spanning the Marne River to Mt. St. Pere, they waited out the final minutes of their daring operation.

The bridge across the Marne lay shrouded in the swirling, sound-deadening mists. It was critical to the operations of both the Germans and the French. Everything had to be timed perfectly. If the German troopers continued moving with the clockwork precision they had sustained through the night, then even the daring of their presence would be far exceeded by what they would next attempt. For they had come here to snatch the bridge from the hands of an enemy force well established on its own ground. A force well dug in, that far outnumbered that of the Germans, was backed with artillery, communications to bring up immediate reinforcements, and had a further advantage of zeroing in its weapons from different sides to defend the bridge.

The Germans, on their part, had allies the French lacked: surprise and audacity.

The last minutes ticked away.

By the first day of September in 1914 the Great War was
still less than overwhelming in its dimensions. The combatants had succeeded in wrecking enormous areas of land,
and at times the bloodletting on both sides was staggering.
Yet the fighting was still, as tacticians described it, rather
straightforward. Combat leaders were to accept specific
areas for fighting the enemy. It was essentially a static-
front war, with sluggish movement on both sides. A
battle of two massive elephants grinding slowly at one
another.

Thus the German trooper who came up with the idea of
bicycle troops, outfitted with machine guns, to serve as a
swift-moving advance guard before a main body of troops,
was actually a man of audacious, almost reckless, thought.
He was flirting with things beyond the accepted pattern
of military operations. The idea was ridiculous.

But the officers of the German 5th Cavalry Division agreed
among themselves that it was *so* ridiculous the last people
to admit its possibility would be the French. Which meant
that if they were too hidebound in their thinking to conceive of fast advance guards on bicycles, then it was most
likely they would not grant to the Germans such an innovation in thinking. Ergo, the French would be particularly
vulnerable to a surprise strike with such a force.

The rigid patterns of men's conceptions and attitudes can
often be used against them to bring about their undoing.
So it was with the bicycle. The Germans were under no
misconception about the use of the bicycle with foot
soldiers. It could liberate them from the restricted pace of
a march on foot, and open up many additional miles to
swift-wheeling cyclists. But that was as far as it went,
where the French were concerned. An army with tens of

thousands of bicycles among its frontline units, like the French, was chained to limited thinking.

For it was the official line among the French military leaders that the bicycle was strictly for transport, and could be effective only when that transport took place under the heavy protection of massed French arms. Logistics, to the French, was the goal for the bicycle, and not exposure to enemy guns that could tear cyclist troops limb from limb.

By this line of reasoning, then, it was obvious that any troops of bicycle soldiers that pedaled away from this protection was doomed to being cut to pieces. They must remain with the main force. This was a fact of life.

Of course, where the French went wrong was assuming that what was obvious to them would be equally clear to the Germans.

The stultified French thinking, and lack of imagination, was the first breach in the defense wall along the Marne River. Thus the German moves began with an already-existing safety factor—the shortsightedness of their enemy.

On the night of September 2, 1914, the lead elements of the 1st Bicycle Company, Rifleman Battalion slipped away from their frontline positions. Advance scouts studying the area until the last touch of day vanished reported all was well. The French had pulled back within their defense positions. There might be a scouting patrol that night, but otherwise the French were holing up for the hours of darkness.

The Marne twisted as it went through the town of Mt. St. Pere, and the main French force had dug in their bridgehead on the north bank. Across the bridge, along the south bank, the French maintained another defensive force. The latter group was intended solely to safeguard the approaches to the bridge. If there was to be any attack against the bridge, the defenders would have more than enough time to both sound the alarm and hold off their attackers, while the main body of troops roared forth from the stronger positions along the north bank.

It was the type of strategy that induced commanders to shift responsibility to subordinates, and the subordinates, in turn, naturally did everything the easiest way possible. As the German troops rolled silently through the night, all protruding pieces of metal were muffled with cloth so that no betraying sounds would alert the French troops sprawled in deep slumber. Only a handful of guards were up, and these few paid little attention to the approaches leading to the bridge.

What could possibly threaten them or the bridge they guarded? The nearest enemy forces were more than twenty miles away. And how could they get there without being noticed? If they walked it would take them all that night and longer, and they would be exposed by daylight, and decimated by superior French firepower. Would the Germans approach by motor transport? Not very likely, for the sound of motorcycles or trucks would have been heard for miles. What about horses? Again the sound would have been a fatal giveaway.

No, there had not been a sound during the night. The outlying posts had heard nothing, seen nothing. So one would be foolish not to relax, to get a good night's rest, to count on the few sentries who had the task of scanning the approaches to the bridge. Morning came, and in the faint light of the new day the world was wreathed in heavy mists from the river. A stillness to make one forget the war. Enjoy the moment while it was there.

The German troopers checked their watches. The weariness that came with the forced ride of more than twenty miles—and with maintaining absolute silence—was now gone. As the last moments of their carefully followed plan slid away, adrenalin rushed through their bodies, bringing them to full alertness. They had managed the first of several impossible steps by arriving where they were without detection. Now they must press that advantage.

The German commander scanned his cyclists, took a look at his watch, then raised his arm for the signal. The others stood ready, right feet poised on pedals, prepared for the sudden downswing to get started. The commander dropped his arm. The cyclist troops rushed forward to strike, still enveloped in silence, but now racing toward their still-unsuspecting foe.

The advance team of German cyclists took advantage of the steep downslope toward the river. There, along the south bank, was the main defense element guarding the approaches to the bridge. They had to be knocked out first. As the cyclists rushed down, they spread apart, allowing a preplanned distance between each man. And as they closed the distance between themselves and the unsuspecting French, they prepared to open fire.

The strike was made in two prongs. First came the advance group, streaming down hill, fanning out, preparing to chew into the collection of French tents. Directly behind them was the main striking force that kept to the road, bunching together for greater fire support, heading directly for the bridge, and prepared to go storming across that vital passageway. The Germans wanted not to capture the bridge, which would have meant bringing up heavy reinforcements, but to destroy it, so that it could not be used by the French to counter a planned offensive by the German army.

Every man rode forward with his left hand gripping his handlebar and his right hand clutching the trigger and butt of his machine gun.

Moving in behind the main force on the road was a third force on bicycles. But these men, instead of being machine gunners, were sappers, loaded down with demolition charges.

The lead team of cyclists rode toward the enemy, waiting for the prearranged signal to commence firing. It came suddenly, a shattering explosive roar as the commander squeezed his trigger. Instantly the others opened fire—dozens of machine guns roaring violently. The men had spread out enough now so that their deadly fire tore into the rows and clusters of tents. In a few brief seconds the French bridgehead force, intended to hold off any attack, was decimated.

Men were killed where they slept. Bullets screamed through thin canvas and tore into bodies. Those not killed outright rose up in panic, rushing out blindly with their weapons so they might see their attackers. They were caught in a devastating crossfire. The men on bicycles continued their dash downslope, firing in long bursts that tumbled French soldiers from their feet, and sent them rushing for cover.

Now they were cut to ribbons by another team of German cyclists. These men had dismounted and set up machine guns to sweep the tent area. As the French soldiers dashed out of their tents to avoid the fire of the men racing at them, they were riddled by the machine guns chattering from the side. It wasn't even a fight. Instead, the cyclists' attack had been so effective, so devastating, that the French troops had no chance to defend themselves. Those who escaped from their tents and from the hail of bullets all about them, could only flee for their lives.

The Germans continued their hammering fire as the enemy soldiers, many of them clad only in socks and under-wear, threw themselves frantically into the river, trying to escape by swimming away, or concealing themselves against the lower bank. This was good enough for the Germans, for their mission was to destroy or pin down the bridgehead defense force so it could not interfere with the main body of cyclists.

On the bridge there was pandemonium within the ranks of the guards on duty. The staccato roar of machine guns brought them upright—just in time to be cut down by the withering fire of the main body of German cyclists, already on the bridge and racing for the north bank. The few guards on the bridge never even slowed down the Germans. Pedaling furiously, they rushed across the bridge and swept up the opposite side. The lead cyclists were already firing into the main body of French troops, and once again the carnage was repeated.

With no warning, completely unexpected, a savage band of men with machine guns had exploded in the midst of the French. Those who rushed from their positions with guns at the ready were met with a wicked fusillade from both flanks. On the south bank, the cyclists who had decimated the defenders were now in secure positions and blazing away with covering fire to protect their men who had rushed across the bridge.

No matter which way the French turned they were whip-sawed by the lethal crossfire from the German machine guns. Badly outnumbered, the invaders had the satisfaction of seeing the French in complete turmoil.

Within moments, the survivors of the French units were throwing down their arms. In the river, dozens of bodies floating beneath the bridge were staining the water a bloody red. Other French soldiers were sprawled grotesquely along the banks, like dolls hurled away and crumpled in anger. The firing began to die away as the French came into the open, demoralized and shocked, their hands held high.

An entire French force posted along the north bank was captured intact. The Germans kept moving with incredible precision. Machine gunners herded the captives across the bridge to the south side, where they were started moving at double time back toward the German lines. These men now served a dual role—as captives and as insurance against immediate assault, for a counter strike against the Germans now would result in thus committing murderous mayhem upon the French prisoners.

As soon as the surrendering French soldiers had been herded across the bridge the enemy sappers received word to go ahead with their assigned job. Their bicycles were safely on the south side of the river. The Germans placed dynamite in strategic spots along the span, connected the wires, unrolled those wires as they raced from the bridge to concealment, detonated their charges. A sheet of bright flame erupted outward, followed instantly by a thunderclap of sound as the explosives went off. Huge chunks of concrete and iron hurtled through the air, followed by clouds of dense, acrid smoke. Moments later the placid gray surface of the Marne boiled with the debris crashing into it.

Well before the gentle morning wind pushed the sudden rising smoke and spray to one side, the Germans were hurrying back to their own front lines, herding their prisoners before them. They moved quickly and they kept up their pace for hours. By the time they were back with their own unit, the story of their incredible mission was spreading like wildfire through the ranks.

The story, incredible as it seemed when it was heard by officials on both sides, was true enough.

The bridge at Mt. St. Pere had been wrecked, blown apart and hurled into the river. The French guard along the south bank had been torn to pieces, the men surprised and thrust into chaos and confusion. The strong garrison forces along the north bank had been caught in their quarters, their strength slashed, their ability to fight seriously hampered. Most of the men were either dead, missing, or prisoners.

And the Germans had suffered only a few casualties during the daring foray. They had fought a brilliant military action and retired safely and swiftly to their own lines. And they'd done it on bicycles.

If nothing else, the French knew how to nurse their wounded pride. The incident across the Marne River at Mt. St. Pere sent repercussions all the way back to Paris. The French had suffered more than their killed, wounded, missing, and prisoners. More than the loss of the vital bridge.

The Germans had rubbed their heavy boots in the French nose. And they'd done so deep within French lines. Let it not be said that the French could not profit from their losses. Six days after the disaster at Mt. St. Pere a French commander, convinced the Germans would never dream that the French might give them a dose of their own medicine, sent a strong force of bicycle troops beyond the French front lines, deep into German territory.

Their mission? No bridge this time. No working up slowly to a specific target. Their mission was to get into the midst of the enemy, who would not be expecting swift and silent mobility—and to raise general havoc. Which is precisely what the French did.

They threw a temporary bridge across the Marne at Mt. St. Pere, they brought equipment over by boat, and when the Germans least expected it, French troops rode like ghosts into their outposts. The bicycles permitted them to challenge strongpoints from different sides, all at the same time, and the French, eager for revenge, were off on a "shoot and run" operation that wreaked no small havoc among their enemy.

Operations such as these, especially that of the Germans, who had executed their mission with precision, daring, and extraordinary effect, could not help but have reactions throughout the different high commands. Within a month of the incident at Mt. St. Pere, the allied armies of the French, the Belgians, and the British had thrown into the combat zones more than a quarter of a million bicycles. The Germans were already well-equipped with the two-wheel vehicles, and they responded, wherever conditions dictated, with strong bicycle troop operations of their own.

Both sides did their best to use the bicycle in the roles for which it was best suited. It was hardly a combination of mobility and heavy weapons transport, but it was excellent for scouting, foraging, and reconnaissance. Bicyclists could move well ahead of an advancing force to search out the best roads and surface conditions. They could study the lay of the land for enemy strongpoints and, like all scouting forces, could often determine enemy dispositions by deliberately drawing fire. A rather risky way to do a job, but sometimes the only one available.

Some officers of the First World War likened the bicycles

in such roles to fast-moving wraiths that always kept one jump ahead of the enemy trying to knock them out. One man on a bicycle, who could use his eyes and ears and get back with his information, was worth more than a thousand men committed to a battle where the disposition of the enemy was in question.

The "combat bicycles" that came into wide use with the allied armies were of the latest designs, equipped with three-speed gear systems that made it possible for their riders to cycle over almost any kind of road, without suffering the injuries associated with the older "hernia horrors." Soon a common sight along the frontline areas was a combat patrol on bicycles, pedaling in low gear along a muddy and rutted road, but with normal riding effort and also with excellent sustained speed.

A sort of "personal combat" flavor arose along certain areas of the front, much in the manner of the jousting that marked aerial combat in the fabric flivvers of the age.

Patrol leaders took pride in the capabilities of their bicycle troops, and fierce—and often fatal—competition developed between allied and enemy bicycle groups. They developed unwritten rules of warfare, much as did the pilots in Fokkers and Sopwiths. At times the exchange of fire between small groups exploded into huge frays of bicycle-mounted forces, as great armies wheeled to have at one another. Finally, just as happened in the air, individualities melted away in the sheer numbers and horror of the war.

Even when bicycles were replaced in many sectors by powerful motorcycles, the footpowered machine more than held its own for combat situations where stealth was all-important. While bicycle brigades hacked and blasted one another in the open along the front lines, commando cyclists took advantage of the silence of their vehicles at night to penetrate rear areas of enemy territory.

In any war, personal stories emerge as reflections of the larger and faceless mass of men who were engaged in the business of trying to destroy one another. These individual tales are valuable and evocative as emblematic of the larger canvas of action. Such is the case concerning Cpl. Walter Roberts, whose bicycle got him into terrible trouble, kept him in backbreaking work while a prisoner of the Germans, and also provided his means of escape—a rare case indeed of a man's fortune being welded to the frame of his own machine!

Roberts was a Welsh dispatch rider who made the unfortunate mistake of pedaling directly in front of the rifle sights of a nest of German snipers. Riding for his life as shots rang out suddenly, Roberts felt the impact of a high-velocity bullet smashing into his rear tire. The Welshman didn't hesitate for an instant. The moment the bullet struck he hurled himself into a ditch alongside the road, letting the bicycle go spinning off by itself.

Roberts discovered quickly, as bullets smacked the ground about him, that the refuge he had selected was extremely low, and hardly the best place to be while German snipers made sport of his presence. Beyond the ditch stretched a turnip field, and the now-frantic Roberts worked his way forward, face pressed in dirt and leaves, belly hard against the ground, hoping to find a shell hole or depression that would hide him from the hornet-buzzing of bullets.

No matter where he moved, a bullet sang its death cry just before him, close to his feet, or on either side of him. It slowly dawned on Roberts that had the Germans wanted him dead by now he would have been riddled from his skull to his feet. They were using him for sport! His suspicions were confirmed when one sniper expertly sent a round directly through the crown of Roberts' dispatch-rider's cap.

He needed no further demonstrations. Immediately, while still lying on the ground, he brought both hands into the air, above the field of turnips. When no further shots were fired, and he heard the sound of German laughter, Roberts clambered slowly to his feet, his hands thrust as high as he could get them. The Germans waved him forward, and Roberts was made a prisoner, at which time the grinning Germans (who could easily have killed him at any time) stripped him of his revolver, knife, dispatch, and other papers.

Roberts' gratitude at having his life spared was immediately modified and colored by ensuing events. Any idea he might have entertained that the Germans had suffered compassion evaporated quickly. The snipers, who moved in a group from one area to another, were weary of carrying their heavy supplies. And there was this stranger on a bicycle. Don't kill him, friends; let us use him!

They did. While a grinning German held his rifle casually on him, Roberts repaired the puncture in his bicycle's rear tire. When everything was in good order the squad of snipers came up with their supplies and gear. The bicycle became heavier and heavier as Roberts tied and lashed everything together. When he could barely stand with the machine, the Germans added a small bag of biscuits for Roberts to eat, and with the muzzle of a rifle prodded him into activity.

Cpl. Walter Roberts was now the private packhorse of a squad of skilled German killers, and watching them at their work made it all too obvious just how slim his chances were of getting away alive. Well, at least it was better than being penned up in a prison camp. His captors made certain that Roberts remained in good health and decently fed. He would be of no use to them as a weakling.

For five weeks Roberts hauled the equipment and supplies of the German sniper squad from one place of concealment to another. Every time he thought he might have a chance to escape he studied the situation with extra care, then changed his mind because the chances for success seemed so dubious. But as he walked and wheeled his heavily loaded bicycle through fields of deep mud, along back roads, and through heavy brush, he never stopped looking for opportunities.

Finally, late one afternoon, the moment came. It was near sunset. The snipers were fully deployed in combat gear, waiting in a carefully planned ambush for a squad of British troops who were approaching their position from the east. The snipers did their job with thoroughness. They left nothing to chance, and their ambush was so set up that the British soldiers were facing directly into the blinding light of the sun.

That could work for me as well, Roberts thought. He knew the Germans had already come to accept his presence as part of their own squad. They were concentrating so hard on the anticipated ambush that they had virtually dismissed Roberts from their minds. As the Germans kept their sights on the approaching squad, Roberts casually began to unload the heavy supplies from his bicycle. No one paid any attention to him.

A shot cracked out and Roberts flinched, dropping to one knee. Another shot sounded. With those two shots, two British soldiers had died. Now the British ran for cover and began to return the fire.

It was now or never. Roberts threw himself onto his

bicycle, leaning far forward and pedaling for his life. Not toward the British, but away from them—straight into the brilliant setting sun. Anyone who looked his way could hardly see him, and besides, the Germans suddenly had a thundering fight on their hands. Roberts wheeled wildly down a slope, swung along a ditch out of sight of the German snipers, and began the long turn back to the east. That night he showed up at his command headquarters, a ghost who had been given up for dead.

Before the long, dreary, and bloody war reached its end, the military cyclist was part and parcel of the vast system of machinery used to carry on the fight. Almost every duty that required transport and mobility fell to the lot of the cyclists—from rear-area carrying of messages to mortal combat in and behind the front lines. Small groups of cyclists grew to complete brigades shipped to the front, and they formed the major elements from which entire campaigns were begun.

By the time the war ended in November of 1918, more than six thousand cyclist troops had met their death in combat; another eight thousand were seriously wounded; and tens of thousands more were listed as missing or taken prisoner.

The cyclist troopers thus took their place among the bravest of the brave.

7

Between Wars

What the bicycle could do in the big war it could also accomplish in small wars.

"Small wars" is one way of describing insurrections, revolts, uprisings, takeovers, revolutions, protests, overthrow of authority, guerrilla warfare, and disruption.

The echo of huge artillery shells was still dying away across the battlefields of continental Europe when new fighting broke out in the British Isles. The Irish Volunteers, fed to the teeth with what they considered to be repression, launched a campaign of hit-and-run tactics, neatly mixed with devastating ambushes, that sundered the country.

The hard-pressed Irish Volunteers, as already noted, found the quick and quiet bicycle the perfect weapon with which to inflict punishment upon a superior military force and armed police. To stand and fight was to invite disaster. The only way to strike hard and survive was to hew strictly to the strategy of hit-and-run raids. The bicycle brought the guerrilla combatants to the scene of their raids and removed them as silently and swiftly as they had come.

A world in which many great nations had been bled white found no way to exist without powerful military forces. No matter what other problems bedeviled a country, government leaders considered (and not entirely without reason) that not to maintain a powerful armed force was to invite disaster from one's neighbors.

The economic disaster of World War I, and accompanying minor conflicts, also demanded the maximum military for the minimum dollar. (That attitude hasn't changed. Today the reference is to the biggest bang for the buck.) To meet these special needs, military leaders studied the lessons of the massive war that had just been fought. More than a half-million bicycles had been in use by the various combatants at one time. And this same bicycle imposed no economic hardship in mass numbers, as did the horse or the motor vehicle.

The demands of peacetime military forces are different from those same forces in time of war. It's easy to see that if you need a patrol to cover thirty miles a day, day after day and month after month, you're going to be faced with a staggering logistics consumption. Using up supplies is only the top of the iceberg. You've got to produce those supplies, purchase them, store them, and, finally, ship them to their destination before they're consumed. Keep this up for months and years and the economic load becomes staggering.

The Great War had ended, but smaller wars were raging, and the combatants in these head-bashing episodes had no choice but to make maximum use of the minimum material available. The strife chewing up the green fields and lovely villages of Ireland was perhaps the best example. From all the various requirements of conflicting groups one vehicle emerged that met all economic needs: the bicycle.

At this point, then, the bicycle acquired its between-wars popularity. Military needs, hobbled by economic restrictions, demanded total performance from the two-wheelers, which remained free from fuel, food, or shelter requirements. Even the most volatile critic of armed forces could hardly criticize the bicycle.

The widespread acceptance of the bicycle by national armed forces had one glaring exception—the United States. The record of the American Expeditionary Force during World War I in Europe made it all too clear that the bicycle was an idler's toy—at least in the minds of our military leaders. The two-wheelers that arrived in Europe with the AEF, were allotted strictly for odd jobs—carrying mail, personal transport in local areas—in general, for use wherever it was easier to pedal than to walk.

No native resistance to the bicycle generated this attitude. Rather, the United States had a smashing love affair going with all mechanical objects that roared and thundered and spewed forth exhaust gases. The more powerful, the bigger, the faster the trucks, cars, motorcycles, fighters, and bombers, the more frantically they were sought. We grasped eagerly at anything that expanded our horizons and increased our performance.

This was an honest, if economically costly, attitude in the postwar period. Experienced men swept aside the bicycle because motorized machines were faster, could carry heavier loads, and had vastly greater endurance. Machines meant heavy weapons moving quickly over long distances. When the argument was put forth that the bicycle was superior in the economic sense, the answer was that economics were overshadowed by the need for performance. There was no shortage of fuel, nor was there likely to be any. It could also be argued that, on this basis of thinking, the steamship was an economic disaster compared to the great sailing ships. And to continue this line of reasoning, the ox-drawn cart could feed itself en route, whereas the locomotive had to rely upon coal, oil, and water.

Such arguments can, of course, become specious. It would be unfair to pass on from this attitude without a word about the philosophy underlying the decision of the United States to ignore the bicycle as a major adjunct to our armies.

We were a nation of vast distances. Europe was, in comparison, a collection of small states with short distances between lands of different governments and languages. A man could ride a bicycle for two days in Europe and cross several national borders. He could do the same in the United States and crawl an inch or two on a map. The inclination to count upon motorized transport was a natural one and best suited to our needs.

For all these reasons it came to pass that between the two world wars the United States kept the bicycle relegated to the status of an interesting experiment, or simply a transport or recreation device, while other nations, combined, put more than a million men on two-wheelers.

Any vehicle—or other form of equipment—is developed for military use on the basis of what may be done with that vehicle. So it was with the bicycle. Experiments had taken place in the past involving the projected use of the bicycle in two-, three-, and four-wheeled versions for hauling rapid-fire weapons into combat areas. The glorious predictions for such machines usually collapsed when it came to their practical use in the field. Testing a bicycle on a paved surface, as we have seen, is a far cry from trying to pedal that same machine through a road reduced to sucking mud. And a man who is exhausted from that kind of effort will soon heave the offending machine to the side and revert to walking.

One of the problems of hauling heavy weapons about on bicycles, when conditions were less than perfect, was the weight and cumbersome shape and size of the weapons themselves. All this was to change in the years following World War I.

New metal alloys, vastly improved ammunition, and air-cooled automatic weapons, all brought such powerful instruments to manageable size and weight, so that their use with bicycle-borne transport became a sensible venture.

The bicycle itself had gone through a steady evolution. Its metal frame was lighter and stronger than ever before. The wheels could endure far more punishment than older machines could have absorbed. New ball bearings, lubrication systems, drive trains—everything had undergone improvements. Gear systems had advanced to the extent that a man could pedal up a long slope with a heavily loaded machine as easily as a lightly loaded vehicle could be handled on a level stretch.

There was another way—a broad view—to consider the military bicycle. Other weapons had improved, especially new explosives. Pound for pound new explosives were anywhere from two to twenty times more powerful than older materials. This had a profound effect upon military thinking.

It meant that one man, or a few men, in the right place at the right time, could enormously affect any given situation—because now they could carry, even on bicycles, a hundred times the firepower available to them before. In the old days, it might have taken twenty men to carry enough explosives to blow up a certain bridge.

Twenty men carrying supplies aren't that easy to hide. They cover a fair amount of ground physically when they're under way. The chances of making noise are greatly increased. They need protection from men who carry nothing but weapons, so their total numbers in the force are increased at an alarming rate.

But if one man can carry by himself the explosive force formerly handled by twenty or thirty men, then a tiny band of three men could do what might previously have required fifty.

The use of such small teams, with their enormous potential for destruction, has made the bicycle all the more valuable.

Among the nations that took the lead in developing the bicycle as an essential element in their military forces were England (especially with its great success in the Boer War), France, and Hungary.

Hungary grouped its cyclists into an organization made up of seven battalions, breaking down each battalion into three companies of mounted cyclist troops. Within each company they established two rifle platoons and a light-machine-gun squad. Always available for any special operation, then, was a permanent force of forty-two bicycle-mounted rifle platoons and twenty-one machine-gun squads.

Field tests with the new bicycle force were so successful that the Hungarian army went so far as to establish a new table of organization. Before the extensive trials that proved the bicycle troops a powerful weapon in their own right, they had always been tacked onto other units. Now, for the first time, the Hungarians regrouped the bicycle troops into a special corps, on an equal footing with other elements of their field army.

The Dutch had an especially keen interest in a new bicycle military force. Having suffered particularly during the war, the Hollanders were determined to maintain a standing fighting force in excellent condition. At the same time, the limited resources of Holland prevented free spending in this area. Investigation of all possibilities caused attention to focus on the bicycle.

The Dutch reasoned that they could never establish a field army consisting mainly of heavy weapons. Massive tanks and artillery forces were too unwieldy and expensive. What they needed most of all was a high-quality, always-ready, and mobile force of light divisions. Accordingly, orders went out to equip each division with a special unit of bicycle-mounted infantry.

Another change came about in the organization of reconnaissance groups. Until the period after the war, the Dutch reconnaissance forces were composed exclusively of horse cavalry and armored vehicles. Looking toward the long run and intent on minimizing the drain on the national coffers, the Dutch army created crack teams of cyclists for reconnaissance squads. Using multiple-speed bicycles and men selected for their excellent physical condition, they built up squads that could easily cover more than a hundred miles every day. In a country as flat as the proverbial pancake, duty in the bicycle squads became a favored choice for the infantryman.

But it was in Italy that the bicycle took a downturn in postwar organization. The Italian army, considered one of the pioneering forces in the use of the military bicycle, decided that the rough terrain of the country, and the long distances separating the north from the south, called for powered vehicles to handle the special forces equipped with light machine guns. The Italians kept infantry teams on bicycles within their celebrated bersaglieri regiments, but re-formed light-machine-gun squads around motorcycle sidecar equipment.

Innovation was the keynote to the use of the bicycle in Russia. A vast land in which the wealthy seemed always to remain wealthy, it was filled with people who had lived on the thin edge of economic disaster all their lives. Until their industrial muscle could grow far more than was possible after the Great War, the Russians preferred the use of man-power to machinery whenever this was feasible. The bicycle, therefore, came under serious consideration.

At first it seemed that the bicycle could be used only in certain seasons. Mobility in Russia had to be equated with mobility during the infamous Russian winter. Could the bicycle be used when the ground was not only frozen, but covered with ice and snow? Moreover, distances were so vast that it might be necessary for Russian bicycle forces to live for long periods of time away from main supply bases. All these problems were seriously considered by the Russians.

The result caught many people by surprise. Using wider tires than were normally found on bicycles, the Russian soldier proved adept at maneuvering his machine over the most treacherous ground surfaces. It was appreciated that men sent into the vastness of the land must themselves have protection, and it would be even better if they could present the unexpected to a potential enemy.

Thus was created the bicycle-man-dog combination, a troika of weaponry consisting of the Russian trooper mounted on his bicycle, with a specially trained attack dog running by his side. It was a dazzling arrangement. Man and dog protected one another. They could maintain the same steady pace while moving cross-country. Exhausted men could sleep after covering great distances, with the dogs providing the best sentry duty. If the Russian troops had need to enter forested areas, what better weapon than the extraordinary scent and hearing of their animals—always ready to open a slashing attack against any foe!

It will undoubtedly come as a surprise to most readers, but the one nation that made the greatest use of the bicycle as a military weapon was Germany. The surprise can be explained by the fact that the German army before and during World War II was famed for its powerful mechanized and armored forces. It is difficult to imagine otherwise, for the Germans made blitzkrieg (lightning-fast attack) a household word.

Yet the truth of the matter is that a great percentage of the German army—before and during World War II—was horse-drawn! *Millions* of horses were pressed into use for transport.

On the Russian front alone the Germans lost more than one-and-a-half-million horses, killed in combat and by other factors.

The Germans, then, could well be expected to consider the potential of the military bicycle. Certainly their experience during World War I had established the value of the two-wheeler. Now they made their move to improve not only on the machine and its weapons, but on the organizations using the bicycle, as well as on different means of rushing bicycle troops to combat zones where their particular advantages could be best employed. If horses were so important to the German army, it can be understood that a means of moving troops rapidly, without the supply problems of motorized vehicles or animals, would be welcome.

The German High Command ordered bicycles by the tens of thousands and rushed them off to training units. Years before the German army committed itself to the combat actions that would trigger World War II, every infantry regiment was assigned one complete company of bicycle troops.

Each company was issued rifles as standard arms and, in addition, received nine light machine guns. Normally, the bicycle company marched and fought with its assigned regiment, but the German commandant had several options for special operations.

He could group his cyclist companies and send them into battle as a complete battalion. They offered a unique mobile reserve. They could be sent out in teams of varying size as scouts and reconnaissance patrols. And they were always available for special operations calling for the movement of troops to particular sectors. Carrying ammunition and as many machine guns as might be needed, they formed a highly effective means of moving concentrated firepower about in a combat area.

Most armies concentrated the use of cyclist troops in two basic areas. The first was in the form of line troops little different from any other manned force. The second was for special operations as scouts or as cyclist commandos venturing behind enemy lines.

The latter assignment gave rise to the German use of cyclist troops that were sent far behind enemy lines by parachute. Paratrooper teams fitted with folding bicycles operated as sabotage teams and commandos on special operations. Intelligence units intended to operate in the midst of enemy country were often dispatched on their missions by parachute, and then used bicycles to cover long distances on the ground, certainly far from where any telltale aircraft engines might have given them away.

Another innovation for which the German army was credited was the chemical warfare unit assigned to bicycle operations. Men who received advanced training in chemical warfare, specializing in problems associated with poison gas, were rushed to the front lines and to areas where an enemy gas attack was expected. Their bicycles were carefully modified. In the frame went a complete chemical warfare detection kit, which would not only reveal the presence of even slight traces of poison gas, but would also permit immediate identification of that gas. Each bicycle was a small chemical warfare station on wheels. The rider carried, in saddlebag pouches fastened to the bicycle, complete protective equipment in the form of gas mask and impermeable suit with hood, boots, and gloves.

On the other side of the world the Japanese were making their preparations for tens of thousands of troops equipped with bicycles to be used on the Asian mainland. China loomed large on the horizon as a target for Japanese invasion. There were Korea and Manchuria in the north, and the lands of Indochina to the south, and in all of these areas there was special interest in the vast campaign of conquest planned by the empire. Japan was a powerful industrial nation, but a small giant. Few people are aware that at the peak of her strength Japan never had even 10 percent of the industrial might of the United States.

To a nation with severely restricted resources, especially petroleum products, the bicycle became a vital addition to the Japanese army. The average Japanese foot soldier was expected to walk to battle, but there would be times when speed was important, and the Japanese wanted that speed without the expense of motorized transport, with its vast consumption of fuel and oil.

By the time the Japanese were on the move in Asia, they

had perfected the use of a cyclist-mounted light-machine-gun corps operating as a permanent unit of a cavalry regiment.

Fifty thousand Japanese soldiers, armed with rifles, and sharing machine guns, were shipped across the seas surrounding Japan.

World War II was about to begin.

8

The Bike and the Blitzkrieg

The role of the bicycle in World War II has been greatly understated. The bulk of the records of bicycle troops vanished in the maw of fighting and destruction. Most of the men who rode bicycles off to war were killed, or so scattered that their stories were lost forever. And in the face of vast numbers of tanks and armored vehicles, of tens of thousands of fighters and bombers and other aircraft, in battles involving millions of men, and in the great struggles at sea, the military part played by the bicycle was tossed aside in the fury of the conflict.

Yet the bicycle played vital, if isolated, roles as an important weapon in a world war that lasted from 1937, with the first fighting in China, to the surrender of the Japanese in August of 1945 soon after the towering remnants of two mushroom clouds drifted away before the wind.

Full-scale war in Europe began on the first day of September in 1939, when the Wehrmacht of Germany unleashed its massive armored divisions against Poland. We have seen how much of the German army was horse-drawn and mounted on bicycles, but it was the very use of such transport in rear areas that permitted the Germans to concentrate their armored and mechanized forces at the tip of their military spearheads.

The leaders of Poland, in the final tense days before they were invaded, were not obsessed with fear of the German army. They respected the ability of the Germans to fight and had no misconceptions about the quality of German weapons. But the Poles could not conceive of the extraordinary discipline and effectiveness of the Nazi fighting forces —and the shock was so great it quickly broke the back of the Polish defense.

As the Germans moved their armor up toward the Polish border, the Poles took stock of their own men and weapons, and concluded that, while they might suffer severe losses, they could throw back the strongest blows that could be directed at them. This was anything but blind confidence, for the Polish armed forces were every bit as strong as those of France and, not incidentally, almost as powerful in numbers as those of Germany itself. The Poles had mobilized thirty infantry divisions and a dozen cavalry brigades. Their air force was on the alert and ready for any action against the enemy Luftwaffe.

What they could not comprehend was the relationship between the armored spearhead of the Nazi panzers—the armored forces—and the long Polish borders. Against the type of attack expected by the Poles—a broad and steady advance along a wide front—they could have battled effectively against the invaders. But not against the blitzkrieg, a massing of the most powerful armored forces on the ground, operating beneath an umbrella of the best fighters and bombers in the world.

Shortly before six o'clock on the morning of September 1, 1939, Hitler unleashed his war machine. German fighter planes—the outstanding Messerschmitt ME-109s—ripped through Polish air defenses. Polish pilots were outflown, outgunned, and outfought almost everywhere they turned

by the superior German fighters. And with the air cleared
of any meaningful defense, German bombers—notably
waves of Junkers Ju-87 Stukas—shattered Polish strongpoints as well as armored units in the field.

And then came the panzers. Row upon row of fast,
deadly tanks. Thousands of men in armored personnel carriers. Powerful antitank killer teams. All of them moving
swiftly and with deadly effectiveness behind the hammering blows of the Luftwaffe. Polish resistance crumbled on
almost every front. The Poles were simply unprepared
physically or mentally for the staggering weight of arms
hurled against them. The Germans advanced as fast as their
tanks could move.

Where the Poles massed for counterattacks they were
ripped from the air, then cut to pieces by fast-moving
tanks. The Poles had no time to adjust to the withering assault. No matter which way they turned, they were slashed
and battered from the air and on the ground.

All too quickly the follow-up tactics became evident. The
armored juggernaughts kept moving. They swept past huge
pockets of Polish infantry, for behind the armored waves
of the blitzkrieg came German infantry to finish off what
the tanks had split wide open.

And within the ranks of the crack German troops, in a
regiment of the Volks Grenadier Division, was a bicycle
battalion hoping to get into the thick of fighting before the
panzers had finished off the opposition.

It was a curious change from the first Great War on the
continent. Then, in the period from 1914 through 1918, the
soldier on his bicycle had been the fastest mobile force on
the battlefield. Those days were gone, and now the cyclist
soldier followed the spearheads of the panzers and personnel carriers into combat.

The German cyclist troops, in fact, never had an opportunity to prove themselves in full-scale fighting with the Poles. The Polish army fell apart much too quickly for that. But there was a vast amount of mopping up to be done. Scattered Polish army units, fully armed and supplied, were on the loose and had to be considered dangerous. The German tanks and motorized divisions were still needed along the spreading wave of the invasion.

Mopping-up operations fell to special units, which included the bicycle troops. Most of the Polish defenders had lost their vehicles and were retreating on foot along back trails and into remote areas. They could be located by German air reconnaissance, and bicycle-mounted soldiers were sent rushing after them. What was important to the Germans was not the destruction of these scattered Polish units, but the need to keep them moving, to prevent their joining into a cohesive force. And this mission the cyclist soldiers did well. After all, the tanks and tracked vehicles would be back soon enough to finish the war. Eight days after the invasion began, the first panzers raced through the outskirts of Warsaw. Less than three weeks later Poland surrendered.

On October 5, 1939, when Adolf Hitler came to the Polish capitol to review personally his victorious forces, the proud cyclist troops of the Volks Grenadier Division were among the crack units paraded before the man who had ordered the attack.

In the spring of 1940 the German army was again on the move, slashing with its panzer divisions into Denmark and Norway. Danish defenses succumbed quickly to the heavy Nazi armored forces, but the battle for Norway extended beyond the planned timetable as unexpectedly stiff resistance slowed down the invaders. Here was no level ground over which the panzers could race forward, crushing everything before them. Even the Luftwaffe was hard-pressed to do its work in steep fjords and mountain passes, where the Norwegian resistance held fast behind its skilled mountain troops.

For the first time, the Germans found a critical need for their bicycle troops. Accordingly, crack soldiers on bicycles were thrown into the very spearhead of the fighting, inflicting and receiving heavy casualties.

Norway was unsuited to great masses of men hammering their way forward. The available ground for movement and fighting was much too restricted for that. The battles became bitter struggles for strongpoints that controlled roads, valleys, and backcountry areas. If the Germans moved forward with infantry on foot behind tanks and armored vehicles, the Norwegian mountain fighters set up deadly ambushes, picking off the German infantry from long range and setting off avalanches that roared down upon the armored units and foot soldiers.

If the Germans were to defeat their enemy, they needed the armor as a spearhead to grind along the mountain roads, while the infantry moved out swiftly from those roads to dislodge the Norwegians. The system of armored personnel carriers following the tanks worked only up to a point. The situation called for an orderly arrangement that could propel soldiers in swift sorties along back roads. The natural answer to the problem was to dispatch selected elements of bicycle-mounted troops down narrow trails and along mountain passes, while operating under the protective fire from German armor.

This is how the war proceeded. The cyclist troopers of

the Wehrmacht suffered severe losses as they maneuvered over icy roads. Yet there was no stopping them. Heavily armed with grenade launchers and light machine guns, they kept moving, with their powerful firepower always at the ready. If they needed to shift quickly to gain an advantageous position, the bicycle was always there. If Norwegian resistance was too great to risk getting into the open, the cyclists remained close to German armor, while powerful tank weapons methodically blasted away at enemy strongpoints.

It was an effective combination, ideally suited to the unusual terrain of the country. And when the battle ended, it was the bicycle—every bit as much as the tank or the bomber—that crushed Norwegian defenses.

Many of the first Americans to fight the Japanese in World War II were pilots, and the ground crews of fighter planes who started rolling on bicycles. The bicycles were not used as combat weapons, but as quick transport, grabbed hastily when the Japanese air strike on December 7, 1941, turned Pearl Harbor into a flaming shambles.

It was a strange quirk of fate that many of our first casualties during the war should occur on bicycles. As the air shook from the concussion of Japanese bombs and exploding torpedoes, pilots caught away from their planes on that Sunday morning took to cars and bicycles, as did ground crews, to reach their aircraft. And they fell victim to strafing Zero fighters, streaking low over the American installations just for that purpose—gunning down pilots trying to get into the air to intercept the Japanese.

The Japanese, as has been noted in the preceding chapter, had prepared 50,000 cyclist troops as part of their spearhead forces to sweep through the Asian mainland. And no military force in the history of the bicycle was so well prepared for its task as the cyclist troops trained on Hainan Island by Gen. Tomoyuki Yamashita, the "Tiger of Malaya," whose forces finally swept through Malaya and into the great British stronghold of Singapore.

Harsh discipline and training, meticulous attention to detail, and perfect timing—as well as playing on the fears of the British and native troops—gave the Japanese cyclists an advantage far beyond that achieved by any comparable force in any war. When we consider that the use of firecrackers along gloomy jungle trails helped convince the British that the Japanese were swarming through the undergrowth—when in reality only a comparative handful of men were creating that impression—it is clear that Yamashita had no competition as a master in bicycle combat.

In the many years of fighting in China, the details of grinding advances and the long occupation often went unrecorded by the combatants on both sides. Yet there is no question that the bicycle formed a mainstay of transportation for the Japanese army throughout China, Manchuria, and Korea, or that Japanese combat and security patrols were carried out by bicycle. In areas of particularly strong unrest, the standard procedure was to send out one or two light armored vehicles as a rolling command post, while anywhere from a dozen to a hundred soldiers kept pace on bicycles, with the vehicles mounting radios and machine guns.

The Chinese, of course, used the bicycle in vast numbers as part of their daily lives, and it was inevitable that Chinese resistance, especially in mountain redoubts, would make maximum use of the bicycle for guerrilla warfare.

Such resistance measures always depended on speed and stealth and the bicycle, of course, filled the bill admirably as a means of launching hit-and-run forays against superior forces.

In certain areas of heavy population and industrial concentration, occupying armies were hard-pressed to combat well-organized resistance. Perhaps the best example of underground organization, making maximum use of the bicycle, was to be found in Belgium. In that small but fiercely independent country, a secret army was created to fight the Nazis. Five hundred bicycle-mounted sabotage teams struck repeatedly at German communications lines, transport convoys, strongpoints, and bodies of troops. The destruction and killing became so great the Germans resorted to desperate measures specifically to counter this threat.

The German moves in Belgium became their standard operation in almost all occupied areas during the war.

Special platoons and companies were assigned to full-time duty to fight the underground. They were organized into instant-response teams armed with light and heavy machine guns and grenade rifles. To better organize the fight against the elusive underground guerrillas, the Nazis kept their units in touch by radio with a central headquarters coordinating all movements.

To maintain high mobility, the special teams were mounted on bicycles, motorcycles, and trucks. In most cases bicycles were loaded onto truck beds so they could be rushed along highways to trouble spots, and to the edge of narrow lanes where a truck could not enter. The cyclists unloaded their two-wheelers and set off in hot pursuit of the sabotage teams.

Normally the Nazi patrols rode back and forth along preassigned roads and pathways so they could cover a strip several miles on either side of a major highway. But this was only during the daytime. Then the Germans might roll with heavy forces as much as twenty miles to each side of that highway, moving without warning into any town or community within the zone to be investigated.

This freedom of action vanished at night. Then the smallest path, the narrowest lane, became an invisible artery for the Belgian underground traveling on bicycles. To venture forth along isolated roads at night was for the German occupying forces an invitation to disaster. Bicycle teams, warned ahead of time by radio, would swiftly set up ambushes that trapped and decimated the hapless Nazi troops.

Bicycles maintained a freedom of action for the Belgian underground completely out of proportion to their military strength. And it was a freedom they used to the utmost, keeping the Germans on edge, and denying them great areas of country, until Allied armies hurled the enemy out of Belgium.

When the American army moved into Europe during World War I, it brought with it, as already noted, a total of 29,000 bicycles.

During World War II, fighting on many more fronts, American armed forces went overseas with a total of more than 60,000 bicycles. But it was a case of history repeating itself—none of the two-wheelers were assigned to combat organizations to be used as weapons. Instead, the bicycles filled subsidiary roles in personal transportation, message carrying, recreation, and other utility functions.

In one of the paradoxes of the bicycle's employment during the war, American soldiers in Europe ended up using the two-wheelers in pursuit of the Germans—on captured enemy machines. Wherever G.I.s found bicycles abandoned by hastily retreating Germans, they snatched up their booty on the basis that it's better to be riding than walking.

Hundreds of G.I.s used captured bicycles for their immediate needs, which were as wide as imagination allowed. After the invasion of Europe on June 6, 1944, and the breakthrough that followed, the American soldiers found thousands of bicycles piled along French roadways. If the French got there first, the bicycles were gone. If not, they were there for the picking. One example will demonstrate a semiofficial use for such vehicles. Pvt. Oscar Mondoza of the 101st Airborne, fighting at the time in Holland, came across a storage depot of German bicycles. One of Mondoza's duties was to keep a steady flow of rations and ammunition going to the members of his unit scattered in the area.

Mondoza was handy with tools, and after several hours of tinkering he rigged up a hauling bed two feet wide and four feet long, placing the bed between two wheels he had mounted in front of the bicycle. The standard rear wheel with its chain connection provided footpower. Mondoza had contrived to assemble an excellent and practical tricycle, complete with loading pallet, for moving supplies through snow, mud, and even across fields.

Of all the bicycles that were sent to combat areas in World War II, it would appear that no one machine could possibly be singled out as a coveted prize by other men.

Yet this was precisely the case in December of 1944 in the area of Manhay, Belgium, where American soldiers of the 3rd Armored Division were slugging it out with crack units of Germany's special SS troops.

During several skirmishes, American soldiers later reported that they had witnessed the incredible sight of one German SS trooper—powerfully built, daring, and seemingly possessed with nine lives—pedaling his bicycle into the worst of the fighting. Intelligence was at first inclined to water down the reports, but the grins accompanying the stories vanished quickly when it turned out that the bicycle-mounted SS trooper was also an effective killer.

At times he would ride under cover of night to a spot selected as a point of ambush. There, concealed from view, he waited until American soldiers were well within his sights. Then he opened fire. The German was an expert marksman. Almost every time he struck, American soldiers were killed or wounded. When the G.I.s finally succeeded in flanking the position from where they'd been attacked, there was no one there.

All they found were bicycle tracks leading away from the scene.

On other occasions the Nazi would ride full tilt within sight of Americans on patrol and open fire suddenly with a light machine gun. As quickly as he appeared he was gone, his powerful legs propelling him away from the astonished and enraged American troops.

The SS trooper burst from heavy snowfalls. He struck during day and at night. Hundreds of rounds were fired at him, but he seemed to live a charmed life, weaving from side to side as he raced away from his pursuers. And still the toll rose, and the stories began to make some sort of cyclist superman of the German. The word went out to "get him."

Even a cat runs out of lives sooner or later, and so did the luck of the German. But not entirely. The phantom killer with his bicycle was captured.

He had killed twenty-two American soldiers with his daring hit-and-run attacks, by himself, on his bicycle!

He survived the war as a prisoner.

It was perhaps a fitting touch that the last use of the bicycle as an offensive weapon against American troops was more pathetic than it was dangerous. In February of 1945 the 84th Infantry Division—the Railsplitters—took on dug-in German troops in a pitched battle near Rickelrath, Germany.

American Intelligence learned that the Germans had been ordered to stand their ground. They were not to retreat a foot, but were to die where they were, or else hurl themselves at the Americans in a final and gallant attack.

And the attack did come—with German soldiers appearing in the distance on bicycles. Armed with rifles and other small arms, the Nazi troops pedaled in an uneven mob directly at the astonished American soldiers. It was an incredible sight to the G.I.s, but their first astonishment was replaced quickly by the grim preparation to meet the weird and unorthodox enemy challenge. At a given signal a withering fire tore from the American positions. Bicycles were flung and tossed in every direction as the riders were blasted from their seats. The G.I.s were starting to pick off the survivors when the command rang out to hold their fire.

The best of the elite German forces had been reduced to

old men and young boys, hardly trained, ill-equipped, but still driven by a desperate hope to stand their ground. The shooting, for this battle at least, was over. The G.I.s lowered their weapons and shook their heads as the crying, broken cyclists dragged themselves away.

Troops of the 6th Armored Infantry Battalion, 1st Armored Division, carrying and pushing bicycles across a feeder stream of the Reno River, Italy, on April 18, 1945. (*U.S. Army*)

Technical Sergeant Albert E. Baker of Company A, 23rd Infantry Regiment, 2nd Division, on his patrol rounds near Berg, Belgium, on January 2, 1945. (*U.S. Army*)

Private Oscar Mendoza of 101st Infantry (Airborne) used German bicycles to build his own tricycle supply wagon. Picture taken in Holland on September 26, 1944. (*U.S. Army*)

A German POW works with a soldier of the 6th Armored Infantry Battalion, 1st Armored Division, to haul a bicycle up a destroyed bridge just south of Marzebotto, Italy, on April 18, 1945. (*U.S. Army*)

Private Ralph E. Litchfield on Saipan, rebuilding bicycles from wrecked Japanese machines, July 2, 1944. (*U.S. Army*)

Troops of Company D, 186th Infantry Regiment, 41st Division, take a break with captured Japanese bicycles near Lake Sentini, New Guinea, on April 25, 1944. (*U.S. Army*)

Heavily armed riot police ready for operations against communist-led riots in Seoul, Korea, on May 1, 1948. Bicycles were used to get the police down narrow alleys and into isolated areas impassable to vehicles. (*U.S. Army*)

Bicycle transport on the move in North Vietnam, starting the long trek southward. The "bridge" is a dummy to mislead fighter-bomber strikes. (*Wide World Photos*)

General Giap's famed bicycle coolies starting along jungle trails to move up supplies for the mass attack against Dien Bien Phu in 1954. (*Caidin-Barbree Archives*)

Military porters of the North Vietnamese army ready to move out with heavy bicycle loads of food and supplies. The porters usually moved in bicycle brigades of ten men each. (*Wide World Photos*)

The famed hand-pushed bicycles of the North Vietnamese army could move 500 pounds per machine. Here a bike is used to bring up bricks to repair a destroyed bridge in Than Hoa Province of North Vietnam. (*Wide World Photos*)

U.S. demolition experts disarming a tricycle taxi parked in downtown Saigon—and set to explode with the first movement. (*Wide World Photos*)

Dead and wounded citizens hurled like dolls about the street near the U.S. Embassy on March 30, 1965, in downtown Saigon, after a bicycle bomb exploded. (*Wide World Photos*)

9

The Great
Bicycle Commando Raid

Throughout this book we have referred to the many occasions when the bicycle was adopted as the favorite mobile weapon for guerrilla fighters, special forces, members of the underground, and other special organizations that moved and fought with stealth as their ally.

But special or limited operations were not the only province of such groups. There were occasions, and we have seen some of them, when the bicycle became a primary weapon for a daring and critical operation on what must be considered a major scale.

Among such actions, the one that stands out from all the others took place in February 1942. It demonstrates about as perfect a use of the bicycle as was ever planned.

Our story begins at night, high over the French coast along the English Channel.

At midnight the world was a silent clash between deep darkness and the sporadic brilliance provided by the light of a silvery moon that rode high along the tumbling rims of snow clouds. The clouds themselves formed a line of battlements towering over the coastline of France along the English Channel. The rushing night wind buffeted the drifting clouds, shredding them occasionally and creating

111

gaps and valleys, troughs and holes, through which a single aircraft and—in some places—a dozen aircraft might slip with ease.

This is precisely what happened at midnight: through the gap of one great cloud ravine, gliding like silvery metallic minnows against the mile-high towers of clouds, flew a long formation of Whitleys.

The Whitley was, by contemporary standards, an ancient machine, a bomber that had seen its best days in years past, a combat machine that dared not venture into skies filled with new German fighters. But while it could no longer perform adequately in the thick of aerial conflict, it flew well, and it had a capacious fuselage into which men, instead of bombs, might fit. And if a special effort needed to be made, the lumbering Whitley could carry both men and bombs.

So it was this night. The bomb bays carried their bulging cases of death, and the bellies of the airplanes were crowded with men. British commandos, clumsy in fighting gear and parachutes. Cold, jammed together, uncomfortable, waiting to plunge into action.

The British formation of bombers was detected by the enemy. German radar, German acoustic detectors, German ears saw and heard the line of aircraft and plotted their probable target. Those targets ahead of the bomber formation were alerted about the chances of a raid. Antiaircraft installations rumbled into action and at remote airfields Luftwaffe pilots hurried with sleep-heavy eyes to their machines.

There was no immediate rush to meet the bombers. They were swinging inland along a course that would take them to an industrial target some distance away. So the Nazis paid little attention, except for tracking, as the old bombers droned over the coastline. And no one on the ground saw the dark shapes tumble from the bellies of the Whitleys. Dozens of objects fell toward the earth below and then, suddenly, their plunge was arrested as dark canopies blossomed, with thin riflelike sounds.

An entire commando force had left the old Whitleys, which continued on with a diversionary bombing strike. The men floated easily and silently through the cold air. They had selected their landing area well, in open fields far from any community. The commandos assembled quickly. It had been a good drop. They were eight miles from their objective. If they continued to move as planned, maintaining silence, there was every chance they would burst with complete surprise upon the Germans.

As guards searched the area, the other men unfolded strange contraptions of metal bars, wheels, spokes, pedals, and handles. Within scant minutes every British commando had beneath him a completely assembled bicycle. Quickly the paratroopers loaded their gear—grenades, ammunition, machine guns, iron rations, explosive charges. Using hand signals instead of voice commands they pedaled away, following a narrow trail covered with a thin layer of fresh snow.

The men rode steadily through the night along the French coastline. Eight miles ahead of them lay a huge and secret radar installation, the most advanced system of its kind. It was a powerful weapon in the hands of the Germans, used for tracking aircraft flying to Europe from Britain. Knocking out the radar would effectively poke a stick in the electronic vision of the Nazis.

Leading the commando force was Maj. John D. Sheffield.

The major crossed his fingers. If events kept unfolding the way they had so far, they could do their job and get out without suffering heavy casualties.

Knocking out the radar installation might turn out to be a bigger bite than they could handle. The radar system was critical to German air defense on the continent and the Nazis were sure to have set up bristling defenses on the ground. Sheffield shrugged to himself. They'd know soon enough.

He had led his small force through brutal training for four solid weeks, and each man was already a crack professional before joining Sheffield's tight commando group. Every man knew as well as did Sheffield the layout of their objective. The vital radar site lay near the village of Bruneval in northern France, about twelve miles north-northeast of Le Havre.

As well-defended as was the radar installation, British army officials were gambling everything on the fact that the enemy would never dream an attack would be launched against the well-defended site by bicycle. It seemed too incongruous, this concept of trained killers pedaling their way into the mouths of German guns.

Well, now they were for it. Sheffield and his commandos maintained a steady pace on their bicycles, on the way to their moment of destiny. The Royal Air Force had flown them in. If they did their job and survived to get away, the Royal Navy would be waiting for them on the beach to bring them out.

There was only one small hitch about that. First the commandos had to wrest control of the beach away from the Germans.

Intelligence advised Sheffield and his men that the radar installation itself appeared to be housed within a cabin, standing deep inside a pit. The cabin itself was located near an isolated house between cliffs that were 500 feet high. The Intelligence report, based on aerial reconnaissance photographs, described the house as "the modern villa type and quite new." Undoubtedly taken over for the convenience of the Germans, judged Sheffield.

Yet the information had presented a serious problem. The towering cliffs eliminated any hope of making an assault from the sea. Long before a small striking force could work its way to the radar site it would come under a withering crossfire. The answer was the parachute and the bicycle.

Even as the commandos rode toward their objective, the old Whitleys were dumping their bombs on a distant target, and hoping the Germans would see nothing unusual in their flight pattern.

Sheffield thought of one beach area in particular. It lay about a quarter of a mile south of the radar installation, a small steeply sloping beach of pebbles and sand lying at the foot of high chalk and flint formations. He hoped to see that pebbly stretch of sand on schedule, for it was there the Navy would pick them up for the dash home across the Channel.

Sheffield concentrated his thoughts again on the defenses of the radar site. Most of the work crew, he had been told, would be German specialists attending to the radar equipment itself. They might or might not be armed. That situation would have to be handled as events developed.

Immediately adjacent to the radar installation, the Nazis had prepared an extensive trench with regularly spaced dugouts, where the commandos might encounter heavy machine-gun fire. A short distance from the site was a powerful pillbox covered by a machine-gun detail and situated right on the edge of a cliff, so that it looked down on the radar installation. Just south of Bruneval was another pillbox. Both pillboxes were so located that they could cover the cove in a devastating crossfire.

Four hundred yards inland from the radar site was a farmhouse with a German garrison of unspecified strength, but believed to be strong in numbers. A small wooded area embraced the farmhouse, which was designated on Sheffield's map by the name of *le Presbytère*.

In all, the radar site was defended by fifteen separate posts, most of which covered approaches to the beach. The others were pointed seaward. Intelligence guessed that the German force in the immediate vicinity of the radar installation—the guard force—numbered about 100 men. Perhaps a mile or two away, the Germans had garrisoned a full regiment of infantry, and a few miles beyond that was quartered an entire battalion equipped with armored cars. Any assault force that moved in daylight would also face attack from German fighters based on fields in the area.

The strike, therefore, had to be executed with speed and precision or the commandos would be cut to pieces.

The commandos bore down steadily on their target. Luck had been with them in several ways. A bright moon reflected ideally along the snow-covered path before them, providing the men with more than adequate visibility without risking lights. And the light snow cover softened the inevitable small noises such a group might make. They reached their first planned stop point, only 200 yards from the bulking radar installation, without any alarm being sounded. Everything was going with clockwork precision.

Staying low, muffling their movements, the men looked to their commander for final orders. Immediately, Sheffield divided his attack force into four units. He would take the first group of commandos in a wide-open assault against the house nearby. The major believed the reserve troops and a good number of the permanent guards would be in the house. If he could catch them unawares—in fact asleep —he could wipe out a dangerous part of the resistance that could be mounted against them.

The second commando unit was ordered to move against the radar installation proper. Group three would cover this move, taking up a position between the *le Presbytère* farm and the edge of the cliffs. The fourth and last unit was assigned to work its way around the cliffs to reach the beach. If any opposition was encountered there, it was to be ruthlessly cut down. At all costs the beach must be secured by the remainder of the commando force for the purpose of embarkation.

Everything was set. The men remounted their bicycles and Major Sheffield passed the word to commit. The first and second groups pedaled furiously toward the isolated house and the radar post. Still no alarm! As quickly as they reached their objectives the men leaped off the bicycles and rushed to attack position.

Sheffield headed straight for the farmhouse door. A heavy boot smashed it open and the major dashed inside, weapon at the ready. No one in sight. Sheffield blew a loud blast on his whistle and other commandos rushed in on his heels, moving swiftly to break into the four rooms on the ground floor. They were all empty. At once Sheffield pounded up the stairs, four men with him, to the second landing.

"*Hände hoch!*" he called, shouting an order to surrender. A single thunderstruck German soldier brought his weapon up to fire. Sheffield's machine gun slammed the German up against a wall in a grisly shower of blood. He crumpled to the floor in a lifeless heap.

Down the stairs dashed Sheffield and his men. He assigned twelve men to hold the house against any entry by the Germans. A fire fight involving the house would neatly tie down any unexpected reinforcements. With the rest of his men, Sheffield ran swiftly to assist the second group attacking the radar installation. They were rushing across the snow when the sound of exploding grenades ripped the night. The men fell prone. A series of secondary blasts lit up the sky. Sheffield leaped to his feet, shouting for his men to stay with him. They sprinted to the radar post, guns ready, only to find that the second unit had already done its work perfectly. The radar post was in British hands.

The second unit of commandos had hit with deadly effect against the dugouts and their guards. Of the six German soldiers who offered resistance, five were killed immediately. The survivor ran for his life, but tumbled over the cliff. Ten feet down his body thudded against a ledge. The helpless German was hauled back to safe ground. Grateful for his life, the soldier babbled answers to Major Sheffield's questions.

No more than a hundred German troops were in the garrison assigned to protect the radar site. But that accounted only for enemy personnel in the immediate area. Sheffield realized that reinforcements would soon be rushing to the scene.

As things turned out, the troops assigned to permanent garrison duty were already on the move. The first sign that all was not well came with a long burst of probing machine-gun fire from the nearby farm of *le Presbytère*. Ger-

man troops were on the move within the wooded area surrounding the farmhouse.

First things first, reasoned Sheffield. Return to the house
and get his men out.

Firing on the run in short bursts, the first group with
Sheffield raced back to the house where the twelve men
were standing fast. Now the men ran outside again,
crouching low and weaving from side to side. The German
troops were completely over their initial surprise and laying down a heavy fire. Miraculously, only one man was hit.
Despite his wounds, he kept up with the rest of the men.

Sheffield's group, joining up with the third—or covering
—unit, scrambled to set up a heavy defensive fire in the
vicinity of the radar post. The demolition team needed
time to set their explosive charges.

"Well," murmured Sheffield when told he would have to
hold off the Germans for awhile, "we'll jolly well give you
the time you need. Get to it, lads."

The Germans moving in from the farm worked their way
steadily toward Sheffield's force. The commandos held
their fire until the last moment, then cut loose with a withering blast at the advancing enemy. As Sheffield had fig-
ured, the return fire from the British force was so heavy,
and caught the Germans with such surprise, that they held
back on further advances and resorted instead to heavy
firepower. Two German machine guns, well protected from
return fire, hammered at the British in the radar post. Bullets slammed into the house in a steady rain of death.

Sheffield was more than content with the standoff. So
long as the Germans kept their distance his demolition
team could complete their work. Then the situation began
to change swiftly. The lights of three vehicles were seen in
the distance, coming toward the radar site.

Sheffield looked about him. It was going to get very sticky in a hell of a hurry.

"Let's get cracking!" he shouted to the demolition squad. "Move it, lads! Reinforcements are coming in and we bloody well can't hold them off for long!"

His words were almost drowned out in another burst of machine gun fire.

"Sir!" a commando shouted back. "We're done! Charges all set!"

"All right!" Sheffield bellowed to his men, sensing that there was no time to waste. "Everybody start moving out! Get to the beach!"

They began moving from the house, crouching low, the men situated in the rear cutting loose with bursts of machine-gun fire to cover the withdrawal. For the first time since they had left England, they abandoned their bicycles. The remainder of their travels would be across six hundred yards of open, rough country, south of their position, toward the village of Bruneval.

But now they had a pack of hellhounds at their heels. German reinforcements had rolled to the scene and German firepower seemed to increase with every moment. It was to their advantage that the enemy seemed to overestimate the strength of the commando force. They moved toward the British in careful stages, covering every move with heavy blasts of machine-gun fire. The commandos were forced to retreat in stages, running twenty or thirty yards, then turning and digging in to fire furiously at their pursuers.

The going was getting uncomfortable even for Sheffield when the sky split wide apart with a terrifying mushroom of red flames. Instantly there followed an ear-shattering crash of thunder. The commandos answered the blast of

their demolition charges with shouted cheers, and an enthusiastic burst of fire in the direction of the Nazis. No
matter what happened now, their mission was fully successful. Another blast ripped through the radar site and an
angry red fireball licked upward, churning within itself
like a thing alive. Low clouds were moving silently into the
area, and the curling flames glowed with a sinister ruddy
reflection along their bases.

Sheffield saw his men staring with fascination at the
blood-red flames. "All right!" he shouted. "The sightseeing
is done with. Let's move it!"

Retreat, fire in short, massed bursts, then run like hell
and flop down in the thin snow for another ripping fire at
the Germans. They were at the cliffs and a voice called
hoarsely. "The boats are here. It's all right, fellows. Come
on down, and hurry it up, will you?"

Sudden elation became shock when German machine-gun
posts on each cliff opened up with stuttering bursts. The
troops in the pillbox had waited out the retreat in silence,
knowing the commandos must venture into their crossfire
when they tried to work their way down to the beach. Now
Sheffield and his men were being cut up by fire from their
front and rear.

"Dig in!" he roared to the commandos.

They had taken immediate hits. One man died instantly
as he took the full effect of a long burst. A second commando tumbled wildly through the air, collapsing with
several bullets in his legs and a third fell with three rounds
in his abdomen. His stunned friends found him alive and
cursing his luck. No one believed it then, but the man
would be carried to safety and would survive the raid.

Sheffield was trying to figure a way out of the mess when
a voice called up to him from the beach. "Don't come

down, whatever you do! The beach isn't secured yet!"
Sheffield recognized the voice of Lieutenant Frost, commanding the fourth unit of commandos. It wasn't difficult
to figure what had happened. Frost's group had run into
stiff German resistance. All they could do was hold on
until more commandos arrived.

Sheffield ordered one group of his men to concentrate
their fire on the machine guns atop the cliffs. With those
weapons pinned down, he led a force of commandos
through the narrow pass and down onto the beach to link
up with Frost's men. The unit firing at the clifftop Germans then withdrew hastily and joined Sheffield.

With full strength at hand, the major began the rush
against German outposts along the beach. The biggest
problem was a pillbox bristling with machine guns. Sheffield and several men with him went in low, against the
pillbox walls, and hurled grenades through the gun slits.
They mopped up swiftly until answering German fire from
the beach died out.

Further along the beach, the commandos discovered a
small house that had remained unknown to them. Within
the house a single German orderly clung to his telephone,
trying to explain to a major from the nearby garrison that
the explosions along the beach were from grenades thrown
by British commandos. Unable to understand the words
because of the noise of gunfire and exploding grenades, the
German officer was reduced to cursing and shouting. He
never had the chance to finish. The commandos burst into
the house and the German signalman threw up his hands.
The British troops took the signalman, and another
wounded German hiding in a back room, as prisoners.
These two men, along with one soldier captured along the

edge of the cliff, were the only prisoners taken during the raid.

Sheffield peered at his watch. It was two-thirty in the morning. The commandos had been on French soil two-and-a-half hours. Off the coast, the Navy rescue force had been watching, spellbound, as the night lit up with explosions and the glowing fireballs of tracer bullets. Finally they received the pickup signal and started in. Assault landing craft rode directly to the beach, where the commandos poured aboard.

Heavy German fire from machine guns swept the beach. Further out to sea, supporting ships opened fire with heavy weapons. British guns raked the clifftops with thundering blasts that killed many enemy defenders and tore huge chunks from the nearly vertical walls.

The German fire died abruptly, and the assault ships pulled away from the beaches.

Of the commando force that rode its bicycles along the French coastline, eight men were left behind. One had been killed. The other seven never made it to the beach, but Sheffield could no longer wait for them. The boats had to break from the beaches. As they headed back for England he counted his casualties. One dead, seven wounded, seven missing.

They were fifteen miles from the French coast when dawn broke. Spitfires flew protection cover. But Sheffield and his men were looking at the beach fading in the distance, where the ruins of the shattered radar installation were still smoking.

10

The Other Side
of the World

First it was China. Fifty thousand Japanese troops on bicycles with rifles, light machine guns, and mortars. A rolling mass of soldiery carrying supplies and food, spare parts and medicines, everything an army on the move might need. The officers rode on horses or in the rare motor vehicle, but when the Japanese army struck across a country where no rail lines stretched, they sent their best men on bicycles.

While the Japanese chewed away at the vast mainland of China, more troops trained with bicycles on Hainan Island under the fierce disciplinary rules set up by General Tomoyuki Yamashita. Others went through their drills in mainland Japan. These troops lived under primitive field conditions. Again and again they rehearsed beach assaults and invasion breakouts. They were drilled until they were considered experts in maintaining their health in humid jungle conditions and knew how to use the jungle to obtain food.

They were already loaded on troopships moving away from home ports when Pearl Harbor was bombed into a blazing shambles. Across the Pacific went the Japanese. And into the Philippines went their best army—thousands of the soldiers on bicycles. Without trains, without fleets of trucks, the Japanese army moved swiftly along roads, paths, and trails. Retreating Filipino troops and hard-pressed Americans were stunned to find the Japanese "foot soldier" always breathing down their necks.

Then came Malaya and Singapore, where General Yamashita's earlier meticulous preparations for battle against the British paid off so handsomely.

The victory he achieved in this theater of war is even more noteworthy in view of the almost insurmountable problem he faced of defeating an army three times stronger than the largest force Japan could bring to bear against the British—and the latter were embedded within a mighty fortress. It is important to note, also, that from the outset the bicycle affected every move the Japanese general was to make.

The first thing not to do, Yamashita knew, was to hurl himself and his men into the teeth of enemy firepower. Open attack was suicide. But what if the defenders could be made to believe that the Japanese attackers were many times stronger than their actual number? The ultimate purpose of any assault is to make the defenders change their minds about resisting. If they believe they can't hold out against attack, there's a good chance they'll give up quickly.

Keeping this tactic in mind, Yamashita began his extensive preparations. Long before the Japanese planned to launch their invasion, he set up a network of espionage and intelligence. He recruited as his agents fishermen, plantation managers, merchants, barbers, and photographers from among the Japanese already living and working in Malaya. From the reports this network forwarded to headquarters in Japan, Yamashita acquired an excellent inside view of conditions existing in the Malayan countryside—and within Singapore itself.

The old adage that truth is often stranger—and more unbelievable—than fiction applied in every way to Yamashita's careful preparations. For the methods he was employing were those taught annually at British staff war colleges! Special studies conducted by the British showed that an attempt to take Singapore had the best chance of succeeding if the invader landed in Malaya and worked his way southward. Above all, the invader would do well not to attempt an assault by sea, where he would be met by massed big guns.

What is so strange is that what was established doctrine in the war colleges never seemed to reach the men who commanded the defense of Singapore, and they operated under the firm belief that the Japanese would never dare to attack except from the sea. At the same time the British considered the jungle an impassable barrier, simply because no large military force had thus far penetrated it.

The rest is history. Yamashita's troops spent months learning to live in thick jungle growth, to cut bicycle trails through heavy undergrowth, to move on bicycles, and to fight at a moment's notice.

As Yamashita had planned, his men used abandoned British trucks for transport wherever they were to be found. But most of his troops moved silently through the jungle on bicycles.

Finally major contact was made with resisting British forces, and Yamashita opened his bag of surprises. First, the size of his force was less important than what the British *believed* that force to be. Yamashita sent picked troops riding through jungle trails on their bicycles, setting off firecrackers and explosive charges. Everywhere the British turned they heard explosions and "shots" ripping through the heavy growth.

The constant "barrage" of explosions and shots, combined with well-timed and fiercely mounted Japanese attacks, convinced the British that they were under assault by an enormous army grinding its way into Singapore from the land side—where its defenses were weakest.

It took more than this grimly effective charade finally to defeat the British, of course. But Yamashita had gained an enormous advantage over his enemy. Large areas of jungle, as well as selected strongpoints, were yielded to his "phantom army," when a minimum of resistance might have held the Japanese at bay.

The defeat of Japan in the late summer of 1945 was the beginning of one of the longest wars in modern history— the bitter struggle for control of the mountainous jungle of Indochina. In the land we know today as Vietnam, North and South, insurgent guerrilla forces had waited out years of fighting against the Japanese, prepared to take over control of their lands when the Japanese were thrown out. The rest is, of course, history.

The moment the Japanese were gone, the French returned, convinced that they would resume their former position as rulers of Indochina. But the insurgency forces of Ho Chi Minh, led by the brilliant General va Nguyen Giap, had already steeled themselves to begin a new fight for liberation—to rid their land forever of foreign domination.

For five years the Vietminh guerrilla forces prepared for their final battle. They had nothing to compare with the great weapons of their enemies. They lacked tanks and armored vehicles, trucks and warships. They counted no heavy artillery among their forces. There were no fighter

planes and bombers. No transports. No fleets of helicopters.
But they had the bicycle . . .

From only a hundred feet away the eye can see nothing
but thick jungle. But as the viewer moves through the
tangling plants and vines it is possible to discern a narrow
trail winding through the growth. A trail barely wide
enough for two men walking abreast. That was all. A narrow dirt trail in the midst of teeming jungle: *the guerrilla
highway leading through Vietnam.*

Sounds are heard along the trail, and a convoy works its
way into view. The word *convoy* invariably brings to mind
great fleets of trucks. Not here. Instead the viewer sees a
long column of weary Vietnamese. They move single file
along the narrow trail through the jungle. Each man walks
alongside a bulging mass of supplies. Barely visible is the
bicycle on which one man can move a quarter-ton of
materials.

A Peugeot, modified with bamboo poles to extend one
handlebar. A brake lever sticking well to the side of the
machine. Racks and handles all over the thing. A bicycle
impossible for a man to ride. But he can walk his machine
with its enormous supply load.

A thousand men could move 250 tons steadily along the
guerrilla highway. Ten thousand men could move 2,500 tons
down this highway. If you had a dozen trails—well, the
numbers add up alarmingly. If you need materials moved
with greater speed, you reduce the load per bicycle, and the
men pedal instead of walking.

Invisible in the jungle. Narrow tributaries. Dozens of
them. A lifeline impossible to choke off. The weapon that
was to defeat the French in Vietnam.

The guerrilla porters who pushed their swollen bicycles

ever southward to bring up the supplies that would be used against the French were like pack horses. Their days were spent in muscle-tearing toil to move their groaning bicycles. Their nights were filled with weary, leaden sleep. When they were awake and moving, their visible world stretched narrowly before them, its horizons the thick greenery of the jungle. Day after day, for weeks and months, this was their lot in life.

At times they crossed marshland or long stretches of paddies. They wheeled their bicycles along narrow trails. They crossed water on bridges made of bamboo and planks. They suffered under broiling heat, endured hordes of insects, and worried about snakes and other creatures deadly to man.

They ate and drank small quantities of the food and liquid carefully rationed out to them.

When they emerged from jungle, there was a vast expanse of plains. And beyond the plains were limestone cliffs. Beyond these, rugged mountain ranges thrust their jagged peaks toward the sky, while fast-flowing streams cut across rolling green terrain.

The guerrilla highway.

If you could stand high enough to gain an eagle's view of the land, you could see for hundreds of miles across Vietnam—a land where the ground rises and falls in steep slopes, blanketed with sturdy trees and lush jungle growth. Only the crude trails of the natives, or those pounded and hacked out by the guerrillas, offer a way through. And even the trails are not enough, for there are enormous gorges to be crossed, heavy rains and mud landslides often make the footing perilous.

Away from the worst of the terrain are the communities. Wherever a strip of land makes cultivation possible, there one finds a collection of the inevitable straw-thatched wooden huts. If there is enough land, a village grows up. Now they can raise pigs and poultry, and on slopes where heavy growth has been burned away it is possible to grow corn and poppies.

It seems to be a geographical chaos. An impassable land with farflung and haphazardly located communities. Not so. There are also deep and beautiful valleys. And it was here that the Vietnamese began to close in on the foreigners who occupied their land.

The cultivated valleys were the garden spots of Vietnam. And it was in these areas that the French settled. Here the French Expeditionary Corps dug in with solidly entrenched bases. Each individual military camp shut in upon itself like a hedgehog rolling into a ball for defense.

The isolated base was called *Facilité*, a strange play on words by the French. At every *Facilité* roads were hacked out of the earth and laid across the paddies so that any part of the local valley could be reached by motorized vehicles. There was almost always an airstrip for transport planes, and, all too often, for a force of deadly fighters and bombers.

The individual bases, the *Facilités*, were hated by the Vietnamese. And the largest and most hated was in the largest of the valleys, located to form a center of communications between China, Vietnam, and Laos. The French were certain the size and military strength of this particular *Facilité* made it impregnable to guerrilla attack.

They called it Dien Bien Phu, loosely translated as "the big administrative center of the frontier." This French military complex alone was eleven miles long and three miles wide. In all directions limestone hills rose in the form of a jagged amphitheater, the peaks crowned thickly with trees, the highest peak reaching 2,000 feet about the Nam Rom River.

Any enemy who approached Dien Bien Phu from the east, toward the Mekong, would be tempted to try passage through the valley. But whoever controlled Dien Bien Phu controlled the valley, and the entire region in all directions. And if he controlled the surrounding amphitheater of mountains he controlled all movement throughout this vital section of Asia.

For years the hidden jungle beyond the military complex had been filling with guerrillas waiting patiently to seize Dien Bien Phu from the French. For years they had been moving supplies secretly by bicycle along the jungle trails to the valley. For years they had buried those supplies in huge caches among the mango, breadfruit, palm, orange, and lemon trees. With their supplies in caves and tunnels, and their bicycles hidden, the guerrillas could mix with the local population, receiving no more attention than the pecking hens or the grunting little black pigs.

Like other guerrilla commanders, General va Nguyen Giap had long dreamed of crushing the French in Dien Bien Phu. Giap was a man slow in his gestures, clumsy in bearing. He affected a loose-fitting uniform without any badge of rank or honor. He had been raised in the sandy spaces of central Annam. The stolid man in the jungle had studied philosophy and law at the University of Hanoi. Even then he was known for infinite patience and an unshakable faith in himself.

Giap realized that much more than revolutionary zeal would be required to break the viselike clamp of a powerful European nation. He studied other men who had done the impossible. He seized on the lessons of Mao Tse-tung, whose religion of military tactics demanded using every means of fighting at one's command, as well as knowledge of the terrain on which one must fight, far better than does the enemy. There was another lesson. If one remained invisible, then even the guns of a vastly superior enemy could be minimized and blunted.

Giap kept to the jungles, bided his time, and built up his supplies. Two hundred thousand Vietnamese toiled day and night, month after month, until the jungles surrounding Dien Bien Phu became an enormous storehouse of guns, ammunition, and food. Giap had waited a long time for the moment now drawing near.

Long before he was prepared to smash Dien Bien Phu, Giap's wife had been arrested and sentenced to life imprisonment by a military court-martial in Hanoi. She had fought to oust the French and had died in a French prison.

Anticipating the battle against the French as it would be fought under the command of Giap, Ho Chi Minh stated: "It will be a war between a tiger and an elephant. If ever the tiger stops, the elephant will pierce him with his tusks. Only the tiger does not stop. He lurks in the jungle by day and emerges only at night. He will leap onto the elephant and rip his back to shreds before disappearing again into the shadows, and the elephant will die from exhaustion and loss of blood."

Following the lessons of China's Mao Tse-tung, Giap knew he would gain his claws and tiger's teeth only by building military strength over a long and patient waiting period. In his land transport was everything. Food, weapons, and ammunition were not enough. They had to be brought to the right place for use at the right time.

Everything depended upon the bicycle.

Giap increased his military force from guerrilla bands to

a battle corps. He formed six infantry divisions, each comprising three regiments. He created a division of engineers and artillery experts. He established antiaircraft commands. And he built an enormous supply organization. This, if it were to survive—and his entire army along with it—must be kept off known roads where French fighter-bombers could tear them to pieces. The rule was expanded. *Everything depended upon the bicycle within the jungle.*

Careful planning soon proved itself. In January of 1951 Giap fought a vicious battle against the French that lasted five days and five nights. The French were astonished at the ability of the Vietnamese to remain in the battle zone while consuming enormous quantities of supplies.

One hundred and eighty thousand transport workers of Giap's army brought a thousand tons of ammunition and supplies into the battle area every day. Unseen by the French, untouched by the French, the bicycle brigades rolled steadily to their fighting men.

When it came time to set up Dien Bien Phu for the kill, the guerrillas intensified their transport flow with bicycles. The soldiers closed in to encircle the great French bastion. Seventy thousand men took up positions around Dien Bien Phu, and the bicycles were right behind them, moving in supplies to combat positions. Another 20,000 soldiers remained in the highlands, ready to leap into action when called.

With the airstrip the only safe exit from the garrison, many French officers drew close to panic, convinced they were cut off from escape. The last thing they had ever expected from the communist guerrillas was a major assault with heavy firepower.

The flow of combat supplies to advance positions began

on March 8, 1954. Two days later the first mortar and artillery shells slammed into the airport runway at Dien Bien Phu.

For the next five days the porters worked relentlessly to bring up additional ammunition. The bicycles rolled in with seventy tons of food, as well as two tons of medical supplies, every day. As fast as the Vietnamese consumed supplies, the bicycles came in relentlessly to replace what had been used.

On March 13, three days after the runway came under shellfire, the final battle began, as the Vietminh attacked in heavy waves. From the crests dominating the valley, thousands of soldiers in latania palm-and-bamboo helmets began their move toward the encircled French.

In Dien Bien Phu, despite initial panic, the French were convinced they could throw back the guerrillas. The natives would be shredded by heavy firepower from the complex of fortresses that made up the *Falicité*. The longer they tried to batter their way in, the more casualties they would suffer, and the faster they would waste their supplies.

Gen. Henri-Eugène Navarre, commander of the French forces in Indochina, committed what was to be a mortal error, in his gross underestimation of what the bicycle could do in the hands of determined men. Navarre planned his estimates of the fighting on the basis of what *he* thought could be moved by bicycle—and it was this error of judgment that undermined French strategy to the point of defeat.

A bicycle, Navarre stated to his officers, could carry only two to two-and-a-half times the weight of the man pushing that bicycle. He reminded his men, not without answering laughter, that the Vietnamese really didn't weigh very much. A coolie at 100 pounds could never move more than

200 to 250 pounds, *if* conditions were perfect.

Navarre, then, was 50 to 70 percent *under* in his judgment of Giap's bicycle supply system.

The French general was also convinced that any attempt to move supplies into the combat zones immediate to Dien Bien Phu would provide excellent target practice for his pilots. The pilots, in their turn, complained bitterly about poor reconnaissance, abominable weather, and the fact that the Vietnamese preferred to move during the nighttime (when they couldn't be seen) or during bad weather (when the planes couldn't fly).

And when the French pilots *did* find evidence of bicycle transport moving through the jungles, the targets seemed to vanish as quickly as the first shot was fired.

The bicycle porters preferred roads to jungle trails, of course. Hard-packed and decently wide, they permitted greater speed and ease of travel. The French planes went after these targets daily. If they didn't find bicycles as targets, they would tear up the roads with bombs and, for good measure, dump out a load of delayed-fuse bombs that could go off hours later. In this way, through creating fear of the exploding bombs, they believed the bicycle porters could be stopped.

Local villagers, sometimes under the prodding of the guerrilla soldiers, swarmed from the jungle with shovels, pickaxes, and baskets to fill in bomb craters. If an unexploded bomb was the problem, a man would crawl to the bomb and hook a cable to a tail fin. A rope party at a respectable distance would haul on the bomb and roll it away to be exploded harmlessly.

Meanwhile, the bicycles rolled on.

The angry French resorted to deadly butterfly bombs. Thousands of the small devices were strewn along roads and trails. They exploded only when there was physical contact with the bombs. But movement on roads and trails was impossible with the deadly weapons waiting to explode.

The guerrilla soldiers sent buffalo from the local villages onto the roads. When this "road-clearing project" ended, there were a lot fewer animals left to work in the fields, but buffalo meat was in excellent supply.

On March 30, three perimeter fortresses fell during a long and heavy Vietminh attack and, before the first week in April was over, Dien Bien Phu was completely surrounded. Now was the time to tighten the noose. Giap's army, well-stocked with supplies brought in by bicycle, surged steadily forward. As the guerrillas advanced, they dug trenches and consolidated their positions.

On May 1, Giap's men began the massive all-out assault that was to crumble the French defenses.

Loss of the fortress of Dien Bien Phu was considered so grave that the United States offered to detonate atomic bombs in the jungle area surrounding the battered complex.

The French government considered the consequences of such a move. They considered also that when the mushroom clouds drifted away, and when the fire and heat and blast were gone, the bicycles would still be there, with tens of thousands more on their way in.

The French declined the offer. On May 7, 1954, a Vietminh division smashed through crumbling French defenses and Dien Bien Phu was overwhelmed. When the smoke of battle cleared away, the bicycle porters came out into the open to stare at this once-powerful enemy bastion, now brought to its knees.

With the supplies rolled to the scene by bicycles.

Made by the French.

11

History Relearned

Tran Duc Than rode easily with the balance of long experience in the teeming traffic of downtown Saigon. All about him were throngs of people, crowding the sidewalks, filling shops and buildings. Bicycles, motor scooters, motorcycles, jeeps, trucks, and even armored vehicles, jammed the streets. It was normal and everyday chaos. Tran Duc Than, like thousands of other cyclists, rode with the flow of traffic, maneuvering among the heavy vehicles.

To look at Tran Duc Than was to see any ordinary Vietnamese. Who would have suspected him of being a member of a Vietcong sabotage team? He looked like any other citizen. There was no way to tell that he carried with him a terrible weapon. Not anything he carried on his person. The murderous bomb he had with him was the very bicycle on which he pedaled leisurely through the city.

Yet there was suspicion of Tran Duc Than. Not of the man individually, but of every cyclist in the city. The 1960s were a time of distrust and suspicion in Saigon. Communist loyalty wasn't something that could be seen. Political unrest didn't stamp its mark on a person's face. Anyone could be the enemy. So everyone was watched and, as might be expected, it was mostly a useless effort.

Tran Duc Than was no ordinary cyclist. He had spent

years in secret training with the Vietcong, known officially as the National Front of Liberation of South Vietnam. They made a demolition expert out of Tran Duc Than. They taught him that his bicycle was a weapon with many capabilities. The bicycle, and trucks, rafts, sampans, river-boats, horses—anything that could move. But of them all the bicycle was best. Vietnam could not move without its bicycles.

In downtown Saigon, Tran Duc Than was a faceless soul among millions. His bicycle was no different from the others that filled the streets.

Not on the outside, that is.

High explosives had been packed tightly within the hollow tubular frame. Beneath the bicycle seat was the main charge and detonator. From the seat ran an electric wire to the firing mechanism.

The man on his rolling bomb could use one of two de-vices. The first choice was a watch and two 4.5-volt batteries installed within the headlight. The second choice was the standard bicycle generator by the front wheel, used to light the headlamp at night.

Either system was reliable, but Tran Duc Than preferred the generator. To set the watch-and-battery system required handling the equipment, and this in itself was a suspicious move in the midst of crowds. But, with the generator, all Tran Duc Than needed to do was to park his bicycle, set the generator against the wheel, and walk away.

The moment anyone moved the bicycle it would explode.

Tran Duc Than nodded pleasantly at other people in traffic. For those who demanded the right-of-way, he smiled. He took no chances on drawing undue attention to himself.

He turned onto Le Loi Boulevard, where the crowds and

traffic increased. Riding was too slow now, so he walked his bicycle slowly along the wide sidewalk and between the sidewalk tables of the French-style restaurants. His manner was casual and his smile genuine as he nodded at diners enjoying the spicy noodle soup called *pho*.

Finally Tran Duc Than parked his bicycle in a milling lunch crowd before the restaurant *la Petite Maison*. Still as casual as any other citizen out for the day, he stationed the machine so that enough of its rear wheel protruded into the sidewalk pedestrian traffic to be a nuisance. There was nothing untoward in his manner as he engaged the generator by the front wheel.

Now it was critical that he leave immediately. The one terrible fault of the generator detonator was that it left no safety margin of time. The instant anyone moved the bicycle the bomb would go off. Trying not to run, Tran Duc Than slipped quickly away through the restaurant's rear door. His haste was justified.

Moments after Tran Duc Than had gone a young boy, having lunch with his mother and younger sister at a sidewalk table got up to draw the bicycle away from the stream of pedestrian traffic.

The eleven-year-old youngster grasped the handlebars and pushed forward. With the first motion of the wheel the generator turned. A spark was created, and flashed to the detonator. For the eleven-year-old, and for many of the people about him, the world ended.

The explosive charge tamped within the hollow framework of the bicycle exploded in a thundering sheet of flame. The fearsome blast wave erupted with tremendous force in every direction. Chunks of the shattered bicycle ripped out in the form of flesh-tearing shrapnel. So violent was the blast that it lifted the four nearest sidewalk tables, including the one at which the boy's mother and sister sat, and turned them into lethal debris. Large pieces of table, chairs, and human bodies exploded into the wide boulevard.

Almost as quickly, the large sheets of the restaurant's window glass shattered into knifelike lethal shards. Dozens of people were cut and lacerated by the daggerlike glass. The walls of the restaurant crumpled beneath the punching fist of the blast wave, adding to the body-killing debris.

The thunder of the explosion boomed along the boulevard, followed by the breaking sounds of glass, the thunder of collapsing walls, and the growing cries and screams of the injured and the panic-stricken.

In less time than it takes to relate this sequence of events, the boy who had moved the bicycle, his sister and mother, and another unnamed person, lay in bloody chunks, limbs torn from their bodies. Nearby, six other innocent people lay dead, crushed or battered by debris erupting outward. Dozens more suffered from blast burns, broken limbs, severe cuts, and bruises and lacerations.

In the street, bicycles had been hurled in every direction. Several trucks and cars had collided as the stunned drivers lost control of their vehicles. A gas tank from a truck, ripped by a chunk from the exploding bicycle, mushroomed a ball of flame along the street, searing several people caught in its path, and setting fire to several more vehicles with leaking tanks.

Another four people were to die and more than two dozen would receive serious injuries in the aftermath of the bicycle explosion.

The Vietcong demolition of *la Petite Maison* at high noon in downtown Saigon was only one of many hundreds of brutal acts of murder and sabotage against innocent civilians carried out by communist saboteurs during the years of the Vietnam War.

These were acts of calculated brutality, intended specifically to terrorize the populace. Only rarely were such clandestine attacks launched against military or political targets. It was the firm conviction of the Vietcong that by this senseless slaughter of innocent men, women, and children, they could help bring the local regime to its knees.

But, when it was necessary, the Vietcong terrorists followed a definite plan, based on specific orders from their own high officials—although what happened looked like anything but the result of planning. During the election campaigns of 1967 in South Vietnam, the Vietcong sabotage teams went berserk launching a campaign of widespread slaughter and maiming of Saigon's hapless citizens.

Weeks before the September 3 election for the offices of president and vice-president, and for sixty seats in the senate, the Vietcong boasted in radio broadcasts that not a single place in the country would be free from death and destruction. Their prediction proved to be tragically accurate.

To frighten the populace into not voting, the Vietcong launched a wave of mass killings, kidnappings, tortures, and general harassment. Leading the wave of explosions that shook the country were hundreds of bicycles packed with explosives. Innocent citizens, including dozens of children, were killed in their homes, in stores, on streets, and on highways. Each day and night was marked by the booming thunder of mines and bombs, exploding without warning. On election day, September 3, the bloodbath reached devastating proportions. Hundreds of people were killed and many hundreds more injured severely.

Fortunately for the favored political leaders, the populace defied the communist bloodbath, and voted in the anticommunist ticket.

In the war that was a mixture of shadowy attacks and heavy fighting on isolated bases, the bicycle served the Vietcong as faithfully as it had served Giap's armies in ridding the country of the French. Thousands of Cong guerrillas used the bicycle as their main transportation not only for supplies but for moving quickly and steadily from one combat area to another. Even had the Cong had a huge fleet of trucks and the fuel to run that fleet, the bicycle was to be preferred for movement along narrow trails and dikes—where motorized transport would have bogged down completely.

During 1963, a British civilian lived with the Vietcong and obtained a rare insight into their life built around the bicycle. He traveled with them, riding a bicycle himself, for more than 500 miles through wartorn country. He was appalled by the many natural obstacles to bicycle movement, reporting on the hazards of narrow winding trails, which included roots, snags, stumps, sinkholes, spikes, bamboo trellises, thundering rainfall, overhead creepers, deadly snakes and insects, tigers, and, of course, an entire air force searching for the guerrillas.

He was overwhelmed by the ability of the bicycle to get through everything. Experience had taught the Vietcong to shun motorized transport. Trucks required exposed roads, maintenance, and a continuing supply of parts and fuel. They could never vanish into the jungle. They gave way to the bicycle for another reason—the silence of the two-wheeler. Airplanes make noise, and that noise could almost always be heard far enough in advance by a guerrilla group to enable them to conceal themselves beneath thick growth by the time the aerial killers were flying overhead.

Against the towering success of the bicycle as a military mainstay in Vietnam, it seems strange that a serious argument arose among North Vietnam's leaders about choosing between the bicycle and motorized equipment for the war against South Vietnam. Yet this unexpected political conflict did exist in the mid-1960s.

The argument centered about the best means of countering the massive military strength of the United States that was pouring into South Vietnam. Gen. va Nguyen Giap by now was minister of defense and supreme commander of the army. Not even the modern strength of the Americans, not even all their aircraft, tanks, electronics, and new weapons, he argued, should force North Vietnam to change its tactics in trying to conquer South Vietnam.

He listened to arguments from his own government that North Vietnam must use modern weapons in great numbers to counter the Americans. To do this, insisted Giap, was to commit military suicide. Not even help from the Russians and Chinese could overcome the tremendous industrial power of the United States, and North Vietnam would be ripped to shreds in the American grinder of military strength.

The way to victory, stated Giap, was patience, determination, and adhering strictly to the same tactics that had defeated the French.

Gen. Van Tien Dung, army chief of staff, opposed Giap's views, and argued for massive use of conventional weapons.

Giap recommended that Dung and his supporters remember what had happened to Japanese and German supply convoys brought under the guns of American planes. Giap persisted and retained control. The North Vietnamese army

went on an all-out effort to move its supplies down the Ho
Chi Minh Trail by bicycle.

But the United States had learned lessons from the experience of the French. The offhand attitude toward bicycle transport evinced by General Navarre no longer
existed. American military leaders recognized the effectiveness of hundreds of thousands of men moving like a sluggish, inexorable river toward their destinations.

Colonel B. F. Hardaway of the United States Advanced
Research Projects Agency commanded the campaign to
eliminate the bicycle transport of the North Vietnamese
army. Among other steps, he ordered that a research project be undertaken by the Battelle Memorial Institute of
Columbus, Ohio, to determine the effectiveness of American commandos operating throughout Vietnam—on bicycles. South Vietnamese rangers would work with the
Americans in groups, living in deep country for weeks at a
time, using the bicycles on narrow trails and dikes to hunt
down the enemy.

The Pentagon viewed the entire project as ridiculous.
Colonel Hardaway was told to stick to the problem at
hand; to stop the supply arm of bicycles streaming down
from the north.

Easier said than done. Every day that our planes flew,
every day that Intelligence reports came in from the field,
Hardaway's headquarters were deluged with reports of
bicycle columns snaking their way southward.

The American military command tried everything to
stop the flow of ammunition and supplies. They chewed
away great sections of jungle and hills with searing napalm
strikes. They dropped hundreds of thousands of bombs,
from small antipersonnel missiles that showered the air
with lethal pellets, to enormous blockbusters that leveled

an area the size of a football field. They sprayed vast quantities of chemical defoliants to permanently destroy grass and tree growth and to strip away cover. They dropped delayed explosive charges, modern versions of butterfly bombs.

But the bicycles kept rolling.

And as long as the United States fought a political war, instead of waging a military campaign, it would never beat the bicycle.

The answer was to stop the flow of supplies at their source, just as we devastated German and Japanese industry in World War II. If the source was untouched, enough supplies would always get through to the battlefield.

And Giap, a wise student of the overriding aspects of politics in war, knew he could count on his source of supply remaining inviolate. So long as that situation continued, the Americans were swatting at tens of thousands of flies with elephant guns. There would be some casualties, but trying to stop the bicycle traffic was like trying to stop the flow of sand with spread fingers.

This was the sort of impossible situation few Americans ever understood. The system of supply by bicycle would always work if there were ample materials at the source. And the United States was not prepared to extend its destruction to the source of supply. That would have meant carrying the war to Russia and China, and there was nothing in or about Vietnam worth risking the start of World War III.

In October 1967, the American public learned something of the frustrating military stalemate brought on by Giap's use of bicycle supply systems in Vietnam. The revelation came during testimony before the United States Foreign

Relations Committee. Sen. William Fulbright of Arkansas was questioning Harrison Salisbury of *The New York Times*, who had just returned from a visit to Hanoi in North Vietnam. Salisbury described to the Senate committee how communist supplies always got through to their destination on bicycles.

"I literally believe," concluded Salisbury, "that without their bicycles they would have to get out of the war."

Senator Fulbright came up straight in his seat with that remark. "Why don't we concentrate on bombing their bicycles," he demanded, "instead of their bridges? Does the Pentagon know about this?"

The vision of a vast force of fighters and bombers hunting down bicyclists in the Vietnamese jungle brought on a response of laughter. But no one laughed in the Pentagon, or in Vietnam.

Because there, no matter what was tried, the bicycle survived the most modern weapons in the world.

In the deep jungle the bicycle—not the tank or the airplane—was the winner.

12

And Now, Tomorrow

Consider the world today. Electronics systems and laser beams. Supersonic jets and men on the moon. Intercontinental ballistic missiles, and robots landing on Venus and Mars.

Where is the military bicycle in this picture? We've seen the part it played for more than 105 years in the military, but at the moment the role of the bicycle appears to be uncommonly dim.

Well, that depends upon your point of view. If your attitude is that of the man who lives in Asia, the bicycle is even more significant than it has been in the past. For awhile the motorcycle loomed as the winner, but the rising cost of petroleum and the increasing problems of obtaining refined fuel have brought the bicycle right back into the forefront of values.

It's in the world of the modern military organization that the bicycle seems to have taken a back seat.

Well, maybe. You need a perspective before you can make a final judgment. Consider the role of the bicycle. It had an enormous influence upon the evolution of the ball-bearing system for transportation. It was directly responsible for the development of the pneumatic tire. It made the need for tubular construction imperative for industrial and financial gain.

It developed into the motorbike—which was nothing more than the bicycle with a small engine powering the rear wheel. And from the motorbike came the motorcycle. The evolutionary path is obvious.

The automobile.

A couple of bicycle mechanics came up with the world's first airplane. Orville and Wilbur Wright. Remember them?

And a pair of bicycle wheels made it to the moon. The mission was Apollo 14, when Alan Shepard and Edgar Mitchell pulled behind them a two-wheeled (bicycle wheels) transporter to haul tools, lunar rocks, and miscellaneous equipment.

The bicycle also had an overwhelming effect upon concepts and philosophies. In practical terms, it is necessary to remember that the bicycle was the first machine ever to be mass produced for individual transportation. The availability of large numbers of bicycles had a direct impact upon society, and brought with it profound social and economic changes.

The whole purpose of the bicycle was to enable man to move faster and with less effort than he expended in walking. Some people consider the bicycle to be a "humanity machine." That's a statement in literal and not philosophic terms.

Consider the energy consumed in moving a specified distance, as a function of body weight. In other words, to move your body from A to B, you've got to burn fuel. If you're walking, you're burning fuel from your body. And you're not really very efficient.

A man walking from A to B burns, on the personal energy scale, about .75 calories per gram per kilometer (one kilometer is about six-tenths of a mile). That's really not too bad if you consider the job the crocodile has getting around on a hard surface. But it's not nearly as efficient as a horse. It's not even as good as a salmon swimming upstream.

Now, from the military point of view, the specific rate at which a man burns energy walking cross-country is vital because supply needs are based on consumption. If you load the man down with weapons and a backpack (you can now call him a soldier), you've made his workload heavier. He must burn more fuel than before, because he's carrying a greater load.

But put him on a bicycle and everything changes. You accomplish two things, and both of them are terribly important.

First, for a given distance, you increase his speed by a factor of three or four. If the man can walk twenty miles in one day, on a bicycle he can cover at least sixty to eighty miles.

And he does this with only one-fifth the energy he consumes when walking.

You've just made him one of mankind's most efficient travelers. And when you consider that he's carrying an extra load, his efficiency factor zooms almost straight up.

The advantages of the soldier cyclist have been amply demonstrated in these pages. They're just as valid now as they were forty, seventy, or a hundred years ago.

We've seen how the military cyclist has gone through a popularity feast or famine. The changes in conditions determining when and where the bicycle is particularly valuable have shifted drastically over periods of only a few years. Its brightest hours came during such periods as the Boer War. Its greatest numbers, as an active military force directly engaged in combat, were during World War I.

Its role as a critical element in fighting a war is no older than yesterday's news stories on the war in Vietnam.

That's today. What about tomorrow?

There are new bicycles on the horizon. New metals, new plastics, almost-frictionless bearings, extraordinary tires—just about everything that's new is applicable to bicycle design.

Don't count out the military bicycle.

It's been around more than a century.

It's got a long way to go.

Bibliography and References

"The Bicycle for Military Purposes." *Army & Navy Register,* Aug. 29, 1896.

"Bicycles Long Used for Military Service." *Bicycling World and Motorcycle Review,* Oct. 6. 1914.

"The Bike for Military Purposes." *Army & Navy Register,* Nov. 14, 1896.

Cannan, Patrick F., Department of the Army, Headquarters, U.S. Army Infantry Center, Fort Benning, Ga. Personal communication to Jay Barbree, April 20, 1973.

Combined Operations, The Official Story of the Commandos. New York: Macmillan, 1943.

"Cycle Infantry." *Hobbies,* June, 1946.

Denny, Harold. "Normandy Battle is Hedge to Hedge." *New York Times,* July 6, 1944.

"Despatch-Riders Give Thrilling Accounts of Their Adventures Mid Shot and Shell." *Bicycling World and Motorcycle Review,* Jan. 19, 1915.

"Die Radfahrtruppe." Official report on Germany's Bicycle Brigades in the World War, Berlin, 1925.

Downey, F. "It Wasn't Always Boxcars." *American Legion Weekly,* Vol 7 (Sept. 18, 1925): 38.

Eddleman, C. D. "Self-propelled Doughboys." *Infantry Journal,* Vol 45: 234, 235, 238, 239.

Engelman, R., Office of the Historian, Headquarters, U.S. Army Mobility Command. Personal communication to R. S. Kohn, Mar. 15, 1965.

"English Cycle Rider Saves French Column." *Motorcycle & Bicycle Review,* Oct. 6, 1914.

Fletcher, Marvin Edward. "The Negro Soldier and the United States Army from 1891 to 1917." Ph.D. dissertation, University of Wisconsin, 1968.

Folsom, W. L. Letter to the Secretary of War, May 24, 1892. Unpublished. Office of the Historian, U.S. Army.

"Fort Harrison, Montana." *Army & Navy Journal*, Sept. 5, 1896.

Giddings, Howard A. *Manual for Cyclists for the Use of the Regular Army, Organized Militia, and Volunteer Troops of the United States.* Kansas City, Mo.: Hudson-Kimberly Publishing Co., 1898.

Gourk, W., Imperial War Museum, London, England. Personal communication to Jay Barbree, Nov. 4, 1973.

Grew, W. F. *The Cycle Industry, It's Origin, History, and Latest Developments.* London: Sir Isaac Pitman and Sons, Ltd., 1921.

Haggerty, Sandra. "A Glance Back at the 25th Infantry Bicycle Corps." *Los Angeles Times*, July 10, 1973.

Heppner, Francis J., Assistant Chief, Modern Military Branch, Military Archives Division, Washington, D.C. Personal communication to Jay Barbree, Feb. 20, 1973.

Hill, R. G. "The Capabilities and Limitations of the Bicycle as a Military Machine." *Journal of the Military Service Institution of the United States*, Vol 17: 312–322.

Kohn, Robert S. "Bicycle Troops." A report to the Advance Research Projects Agency, Department of Defense, Washington, D.C., as ordered prepared by the Battelle Memorial Institute, Columbus, Ohio, Sept. 30, 1965.

Lawton, E. P. "The Bicycle in Military Use." *Journal of the Military Service Institution of the United States*, Vol 21 (1897): 449–461.

May, William T. *Cyclists' Drill Regulations, United States Army.* Boston: Pope Manufacturing Co., 1892.

Miles, Nelson A. "Annual Report," Headquarters, Department of the Missouri, Chicago, Illinois. Sept. 4, 1892.

"Military Cycling." Speech written by Maj. Gen. Nelson A. Miles, 1892.

Moss, James A. "Report of a Bicycle Trip from Fort Missoula, Montana, to St. Louis, Missouri." *Army & Navy Journal*, Sept. 1, 1897.

Nankivell, John H., ed. *History of the 25th Regiment United States Infantry from 1869 to 1926.* Denver: Smith-Books Printing Co., 1927.

"A New Military Folding Bicycle." *Scientific American*, Vol 83, Oct. 20, 1900.

"Note on the Cyclist Brigade (Germany)." Memorandum prepared by M.I.2, Postive Branch, Military Intelligence Division, General Staff, United Kingdom, Nov. 23, 1918.

Ordway, Albert. *Cycle-Infantry Drill Regulations of the District of Columbia National Guard.* Washington, D.C.: Judd and Detweiler, 1892.

Palmer, Arthur Judson. *Riding High, The Story of the Bicycle.* New York: Dutton, 1957.

"Report of Evaluation Tote Gote Test in Thailand." Summary Report, Vol I, Joint Thai-United States Military Research and Development Center, Bangkok, Thailand, Dec. 1964.

Rippenbein, A. P., President, Bicycle Built-in-Two, Inc. Letter to the Quartermaster General on folding bicycles, Sept. 26, 1941.

Roy, J. *The Battle of Dien Bien Phu.* New York: Harper, 1965.

Sheffield, J. D. "A Commando-Cyclist's Letter to His Son." London: Imperial War Museum, 1943.

Slonaker, John J., Research Historian, Department of the Army, U.S. Army Military History, Research Collection, Carlisle Barracks, Pa. Personal communication to Jay Barbree, April 27, 1973.

Slonaker, John J., Research Historian, Department of the Army, U.S. Army Military History Research Collection, Carlisle Barracks, Pa. Personal communication to Jay Barbree, May 14, 1973.

Tables of Organization. Washington, D.C.: U.S. War Department, 1914.

Thomas, Audrey E., Magazine and Book Branch, Directorate for Defense Information, Assistant Secretary of Defense, Washington, D.C. Personal communication to Jay Barbree, Feb. 6, 1973.

Thompson, J. B. "Changes in Cavalry and Developments in Mechanization in France, Great Britain, Germany, Italy, Russia, and Japan, with Trends in Those Arms." Paper, U.S. Army War College, Fort Humphreys, D.C., May 10, 1938.

"25th U.S. Infantry Bicycle Corps." *Army & Navy Journal*, July 3, 1897.

"25th U.S. Infantry Bicycle Corps." *Army & Navy Journal*, July 31, 1897.

"25th U.S. Infantry Bicycle Corps." *Army & Navy Journal*, Aug. 7, 1897.

"25th U.S. Infantry Bicycle Corps." *Army & Navy Journal*, Oct. 2, 1897.

"United States Army in the World War, 1917–1919: Organization of the American Expeditionary Forces." Washington, D.C.: U.S. Army Historical Division, 1948.

Whitney, Henry H. "The Adaptation of the Bicycle to Military Uses." *Journal of the Military Service Institution of the United States,* Vol 17 (1895): 542–563.

"With the Cyclists in the Fields of Battle." *Bicycling World and Motorcycle Review,* Oct. 6, 1914.

Index

American Expeditionary Force,
21–22, 88
American Wheelman's Association (AWA), 16
Anderson, James C., 41

Ball bearing systems, 40, 90, 147
Battelle Memorial Institute of
Columbus (Ohio), 144
Belgian Army, 21, 22, 80, 105,
106
Bersaglieri rifle battalions, 13,
38, 92
Bicycle ambulance, 19
Biscuit-and-Bean March, 43–59
beginning of, 43–46
end of, 58–59
first stop, 46–47
route of, 44, 46
supplies and equipment, 45–46
weather conditions, 47
Black-and-Tans (British police
force), 24–25
Blitzkrieg, 94, 98–110
invasion of Poland, 98–101
Boer War, 20–21, 64–68, 91
beginning of, 64–65
end of, 67–68
guerrilla operations, 67

British Army, 21, 80
Bruneval commando raid, 111–
123
beginning of, 116–117
casualties, 123
demolition charges, 121
intelligence operations, 114–
115
Nazi pillbox installations,
115–116
prisoners-of-war, 122–123
Butterfly bombs, 135–136

Cheyenne Indians, 53
China, 104–105
Chiricahua Apaches, 17
Christy saddles, 45
Colt automatic machine guns, 19
Cook, Private, 45
Crow Indian Reservation, 51
Cuba, U.S. occupation of (1898),
20

Davidson, Maj. R. P., 18, 19
Demolition squads, 22
Denmark, invasion of (1940),
101–102
Dien Bien Phu, battle of, 11, 30,
130–131, 132–136